GRACE AND TRUTH

Grace Lightfoot Faus, 1955

GRACE AND TRUTH

THE STORY OF
GRACE LIGHTFOOT FAUS

Ordained Minister
In The Nation's Capital

Lula Zevgolis

DeVorss & Company
Box 550
Marina del Rey, California 90294

ISBN: 0-87516-541-9
Library of Congress Catalog Card Number: 84-71619

Cover design by Irene Zevgolis

Printed in the United States of America

The author wishes to express
her deep appreciation to
Mrs. Norene M. Diamond
Miss Marjorie B. Colvin
Mr. Gerald Loubier
and
Mrs. Hedda Lark of DeVorss & Company
for their invaluable assistance
in the preparation of this book

To
Emmanuel, Frank, and Irene

CONTENTS

Foreword, by Dr. Ervin Seale

FOREWORD

While reading the galleys of these pages, my eye fell frequently upon an ancient printed symbol lying on the table in front of me. It was the numbers 6 and 9 in one design. Looked at from the top it was the figure 6, representing in ancient lore the descent of the spirit into matter or form. Looked at from the bottom it is the figure 9, representing the ascent of spirit out of matter.

Seeing this symbol before me while reading about the physical history of Dr. Faus, was an experience of what C. G. Jung calls *synchronicity* — two seemingly unrelated things happening at the same time. Life is full of them. But of course they are not unrelated. My Meta always accompanies my form. There is only One Being, One Mind, One Nature, having an individual and distinctive experience in four billion different human ways and personalities. Grace first learned it under the name of *Omnipresence*, and she has been demonstrating it ever since.

Anyone who has known Grace Faus has a ready-made interest in the story of her life, and the suspense of the narrative increases that interest. The girl from Cripple Creek has come a long way. We all like to know the answers to "What made her tick?" and "How did she do it?"

I began my reading of *Grace and Truth* in this way, but was soon enthralled by another story that kept overshadowing the first one. On my table the symbol kept speaking to me that the letters on the page did not tell the whole story; that this was not just another biography, a tale of human beings; that this was the old, old story, perennial with the ages. Repeated over and over, yet ever new — here is the story of the Eternal Wayfarer, remembering herself, descending into hell if necessary, but always transcendent. And it never ends. One figure in the symbol blends and modulates into the other. Beholding it, we are constrained to say, "Amazing Grace!"

ERVIN SEALE

New York, N. Y.
February 1985

THE LAW WAS GIVEN BY MOSES,
BUT GRACE AND TRUTH CAME BY
JESUS CHRIST.

John 1:17

CHAPTER I

COLORADO GOLD

The year was 1892, and the main topic of conversation in the engineering office of the Santa Fe Railway in Topeka, Kansas, was gold — the prize that lured men's hearts, mesmerized their minds, and bid them pull up stakes to join the hordes hurrying west in search of the riches rumored to be buried in the vast virgin territory of the Colorado mountains.

Running a close second was the subject of the political and economic plight of the country. Benjamin Harrison's term was drawing to a close in a storm of political unrest paralleled by rumors that the nation was swiftly sliding into an acute industrial and economic depression.

In the office he shared with Frank Jeffries, William Lightfoot lifted his head from the maps spread out on his drafting table and looked out the window. He laughed, then walked to the open doorway, shaking his head.

Rounding the bend in the road less than thirty yards away trudged an old prospector, goading his burro as he plodded along with his tent, blanket, bag, frying pan, pick and shovel.

Lightfoot grinned as he stood watching the traveler until he disappeared from sight.

Following his partner's gaze, Frank Jeffries moved to the window.

"Well, there goes another one! *Pike's Peak or bust!*"

"I hope he strikes it rich," William Lightfoot remarked. "He deserves to."

"What do you say, Bill? How about it? When are *we* going?"

"Nothing doing! I've got enough to keep me busy *above* ground! No need to go digging for more."

"Who said anything about *digging*? Seriously, Bill, I've been giving it some thought. I'm sort of—sold on Cripple Creek. Tom Flynn was up there with the Leadville crew and he claims the place is loaded. He says people are hightailing it into that area at around a thousand a month—swarming over those hills like flies! But the real gold mine for you and me would be a surveying office smack in the middle of that whole district! Those men pouring into that camp with their families have got to have homes, grocery stores, pharmacies, doctors' and lawyers' offices, churches, and schools to accommodate them. They need *surveyors*, Lightfoot! Surveyors to plat the townsite, the lots, the entire district. Cripple Creek's a babe-in-arms, Bill. Surveying that area would be a bonanza in itself. Think about it. Think about it seriously, Bill. I'm ready to go whenever you are!"

William Lightfoot sat forward on his stool, his elbows supporting his tall frame as he leaned against the table, and with a sweep of his hand scooped up the brush he used for whisking away erasure crumbs. He looked up slowly and scanned the confines of the small office—the cabinet that held his telescope and compass case; his transit folded and propped in the corner, his extra pair of leather boots alongside; the maps, rolled and tied, huddled in the corner near the window; the plat books stacked on the shelf; his drawing instruments lying in the open case on his drafting board; his log book filled with figures.

"Come off it, Frank. Grace would never agree to it. Besides, there's Fairy to think about. She's only five, you know. You haven't started raising a family yet. When you do, you'll not be so ready to pick up and go!"

"Bill, Fairy's as sturdy as a pine knot! And Grace—well, *Mary* is willing, and Grace is as game a girl as Mary."

"You can't be serious, Frank. That part of Colorado is a wilderness. You'd need a corps of axe men to get you through to the place."

"No, no—not anymore. That's ranch country out there now—pretty well developed, at that. Cripple Creek lies in a valley just west of Pike's Peak. Tom Flynn told me it got its crazy name from a *cow*! The story goes that the first cattlemen to settle in that valley were building a shelter to protect their spring from pollutants and wild game. A log slipped, hit somebody, and caused his gun to go off. A panicky calf scuttling to clear out in a hurry tried to jump across the creek and broke its leg falling into the creek bed. When the commotion was over, the boss of the bunch was supposed to have yelled, 'Well boys, *this here's sure some cripple creek!*'"

Lightfoot shook his head. Jeffries reached over to the window ledge for the *Topeka Capital* and began shuffling through its pages.

"Cripple Creek is not as remote as you think, Bill. Actually it's quite accessible. There's rail service now within eighteen miles of the place. Here. Take a look at this."

He folded the paper over and handed it to his partner. A Colorado Midland Railway advertisement read:

CRIPPLE CREEK is not only a HEALTH but
a WEALTH resort.
Location near PIKE'S PEAK.
GOLD. Bright yellow gold is found

4

at grass roots in the rock formation.
Reliable experts claim that this is
today the richest gold camp in Colorado.
Assays average over $100 per ton, and
have run as high as FIVE THOUSAND DOLLARS.
100 people per day are now rushing into
this DISTRICT.
A chance of a lifetime is worth looking after.
The ONLY WAY to reach CRIPPLE CREEK is via
FLORISSANT and THE COLORADO MIDLAND RAILWAY.
Inquire of Local agents for particulars, or Chas. S. Lee, gen'l.
passenger agent, Denver, Colo.

William Lightfoot refolded the *Capital* and handed it back
to Jeffries.

"Well, what do you say, Bill?"

"I say that's a pretty good piece of advertising propagan-
da," Lightfoot answered with a wry smile. He turned to his
drawing board, picked up a pencil, and bent over his maps
once more.

It was neither Frank Jeffries' enthusiasm nor the colorful
Colorado Midland Railway advertisement that spurred
William Lightfoot into planning to set out for Cripple Creek,
Colorado, with his family five months later. It was, rather, the
stark reality of a nationwide depression and its devastating effect on the agriculturally-based economy of Kansas. Too, it
was William's careful weighing of rumors rising midst increasing lay-offs and salary cuts in the Santa Fe offices that the
Railway System for which he worked was fast approaching the
end of its line and would declare bankruptcy within the year.

Only six days remained now until the Lightfoots would
leave Topeka for Cripple Creek with Mary and Frank Jeffries.
The two families had taken grateful hold of news that in Crip-

ple Creek business was booming. Reportedly, things were so lively in that gold-mining town that staffs of hastily-contrived services were working overtime to meet the demand. Moreover, the fame-gaining gold camp was so preoccupied with its riches that its citizens were hardly aware of the desperate conditions plaguing the rest of the country and had little time to wonder or ask.

"I keep wondering what it will be like, William — living in a gold camp," Grace Lightfoot remarked to her husband.

William withheld comment. He knew only too well what it would be like. But he dared not risk his wife's reaction now to reports that whiskey and beer rolled into Cripple Creek by the barrel; that raucous street brawls took place hourly as flaring tempers vied for land tracts and claims control, share sales and rights transfer deals; that enterprising madams and their girls managed parlor houses and cribs in Cripple Creek's notorious red-light district; that gambling stakes soared nightly in dance halls to banged-out versions of "There'll be a Hot Time In the Old Town Tonight," the tune that was sweeping the country, created in Cripple Creek and inspired by the gold camp's night-time antics.

Wild is what it will be like, William thought ruefully. *Absolutely wild.*

Their remaining days in Topeka dwindled to three, then two. Suddenly, the time for departure had come.

The sun shone bright and and the air was crisp that afternoon in September of 1893 when they boarded the *Santa Fe* at the Topeka station for Colorado Springs, Colorado. The train lurched forward at 1:05, its cars banging and straining against each other as the wheels ground into motion. The Lightfoots and the Jeffrieses leaned back in their seats then, faced with the finality of their decision to leave Topeka. There was no turning back now. They were rolling along on their way to Cripple Creek.

It was eight o'clock the next morning when they stepped down from the Santa Fe's platform in Colorado Springs to change to the *Colorado Midland* for Florissant. Crumpled and weary, they waited then in Florissant for the stagecoach that would take them the remaining eighteen miles to Cripple Creek.

The coach was a welcome sight as it swayed to a stop at the station, signaling the last lap of their journey. William Lightfoot and Frank Jeffries helped their women onto the creaky stage, which was already crowded with dusty prospectors smelling of stale tobacco and soiled clothing.

Grace Lightfoot held her child close as the coach pitched forward, jolting and jostling them about, its wheels creaking and grinding over the rutted, rocky road. They rolled along in a cloud of dust as the horses pulled them down the narrow roadway that twisted before them through stretches of densely overgrown hill country.

The way appeared increasingly treacherous and Grace became filled with misgivings. The surrounding country looked primitive, far removed from civilization. They were in the midst of a wilderness! She fought a sense of panic. What had possessed her to agree to such a thing? She wished she were back in Topeka. There she would gladly settle for what little there was to be had. Cripple Creek was an opportunity, William had persuaded her—a tremendous opportunity to get ahead. It was, William had agreed with Frank Jeffries, the best possible place for them to ride out the depression.

In her secure world, it had seemed to Grace that the depression had crept up on them stealthily, like a thief in the night. Actually, the nation's sick economy had been long in the making, stemming back to the 1880's.

Throughout the decade, political, industrial, and economic crisis piled upon crisis until, two months after

Grover Cleveland's inauguration, the bottom dropped out of everything. Now, the nation lay paralyzed by the Great Panic of 1893.

Mary Jeffries nudged Grace, and Grace looked at her nervously.

"This was Ute territory not long ago," Mary said softly, peering out the window. "The Utes were notoriously hostile."

Frank Jeffries caught his wife's words and noted the concern on the women's faces.

"Easy, girls. The Utes have been on reservations farther west since 1888. You won't see a one. Anyway, with a name like *Lightfoot* among us, we'd pass approved. What tribe do you stem from, anyway, Bill? *Lightfoot's* got to be Indian."

"Not a bit," William replied with a grin. "Believe it or not, it's pure English."

They were at the top of the hill overlooking Cripple Creek now. The horses, stopping after the long haul up the incline, stood pawing the ground. Then they bolted down the hill and into the town, sliding to a stop in front of the Continental Hotel.

A barrage of whistles, shouts, and pistol cracks went up from the crowd that had gathered to welcome the day's tardy stage. The passengers looked at each other blank-faced as they stepped down from the coach. Yet the goodwill and friendly cheer that had triggered the unnerving racket reassured them somehow and lightened their weariness. Clutching their baggage, the newcomers found themselves smiling and nodding in greeting as they moved through the pressing throng.

CHAPTER II

GRACE ELEANOR LIGHTFOOT

The Lightfoots and the Jeffrieses settled in cabins a few yards from each other on Poverty Gulch near the shack of Bob Womack, Cripple Creek's pioneer prospector and the first in the camp to discover gold.

Conditions in the camp were shockingly primitive. The two young wives compared notes, and mustering all their courage, decided that there was only one thing to do about the circumstances of their new environment and that was to make the best of them. This they did independently of their husbands, who were inextricably involved in establishing their new office on Cripple's main thoroughfare.

It was mid-autumn now and the leaves of the aspens glinted gold in the brilliant sunlight, drifting down to settle in bright, quilt-like patches over the green and ochre hills. There was a snap to the air at that exhilarating height of nearly ten thousand feet that the young newcomers liked. The camp was located in a beautiful valley near the western slopes of Pike's Peak just below timberline, fringed on the south by the snow-laced crests of the Sangre de Cristo Mountains while to the west lay the Continental Divide. The gulched valley with its centrally-winding stream was surrounded by spruce-clumped foothills. It was exciting to see new people flock into the district daily and the two young women watched in amazement as the mushrooming town expanded toward neighboring Mt. Pisgah, named by an early traveler for the famed biblical mountain.

Mary and Grace bought their drinking water from water wagons, and, when they needed supplies, walked the most direct route down Poverty Gulch to the business section on Bennett Avenue. They scrupulously averted their eyes at the Myers Avenue intersection, an artery teeming with saloons, gambling houses, dance halls, and parlor houses—most notably the two-story red brick residence known as *The Old Homestead*.

The newcomers were not long in residence when a diphtheria outbreak swept the camp. When the epidemic subsided and danger of contagion had passed, Grace began to go to church Sundays. A staunch Methodist, she had been disappointed to find no Methodist group in the camp. As an alternative, she attended the Congregational services on Carr Avenue held in a large tent called "WHOSOEVER WILL."

Sometime later a dynamic young minister arrived in Cripple Creek to establish the Methodist church there, and the Lightfoots were soon among his most dedicated parishioners. William and Grace were never to know that the grandson of this pioneer churchman, Dr. Max H. Ballard, would one day succeed their younger daughter as she retired from her unique profession in life.

Grace thought less frequently now of Topeka and what life had held for her there. She had made her peace with Cripple Creek. When she did think of Topeka it was almost as if it were another world. Yet Topekans along with the rest of the country were very much aware of Cripple Creek. The gold camp was a coast-to-coast conversation piece, firing imaginations everywhere.

"BOOM, CRIPPLE!" echoed throughout the land as *Cripple Creek* became synonymous with prosperity and riches, and was given the title of "The World's Greatest Gold Camp."

In the midst of Cripple's heady success the surveying team of Lightfoot and Jeffries was so hard-pressed to keep up with demands for surveying and resurveying that the two men often mapped and platted far into the night, preparing urgent documents on which lawsuits pended. Too, they burned the midnight oil mapping mine property boundaries so that mine owners could apply quickly for claim patents.

Winding up such a project late one night, William Lightfoot laid down his pencil and rose to answer a knock at the door. William Shemwell stood there, disheveled, fatigued.

"Come in, Bill," Grace Lightfoot heard her husband say as she lay reading behind the closed door of the bedroom.

"Thanks, Lightfoot. It's awful late, so I'll get right to it," Shemwell began. "Look, Bill, I need some surveying done. I'll give you a share in my mine if you'll survey it for me. It's got to be done right away and it's the only way I can manage it right now. How about doing the job for me for half-interest?"

William had come to know Bill Shemwell out on the hill. He looked at his friend now and shook his head slowly.

"That's gambling, Bill. I won't do it."

"*Gambling*? What do you mean, *gambling*? The Elkton's a sure thing! Now you mark my words! I'm giving you first option, Lightfoot. Any surveyor in this camp would jump at the chance!"

"I appreciate it, Shemwell. Thanks. But I can't do it. I'll credit you, if you want."

"Nah, no. Well, that's that, Lightfoot. No hard feelings. Just thought you might be interested. Well, good-night."

The door closed behind him and Grace burst out of the bedroom wide-eyed and incredulous.

"William! William, for heaven's sake! Why didn't you do it? Half interest in a gold mine! That's a once-in-a-lifetime op-

portunity! Why—why, you don't know—it could make us rich!"

William Lightfoot's eyes met his wife's gaze evenly. Grace read their message and said no more.

But through the years she kept an eye open and an ear tuned for news of the Elkton mine. When it joined the ranks of the gold camp's leading producers, Grace Lightfoot censured her husband for denying her a place in Cripple's upper strata of wealth and society. Exasperatingly contriteless, William heard her out and went his usual busy way.

Then in the crisp of a Cripple Creek autumn Grace learned she was carrying their second child.

"According to Dr. Whiting the baby will be born about mid-May," Grace Lightfoot wrote to her parents, Eleanor and Henry Strong, in April of '97. "If it's a boy he'll be named William Henry Lightfoot, for the two great men in my life."

"A name a man can be proud of," Henry Strong wrote back to his daughter. "If it's a girl, name her for the two great women in *my* life — Eleanor and Grace."

"I'll go along with that," William Lightfoot said, "provided *my* lady places first."

Grace Eleanor Lightfoot was born at two o'clock the afternoon of May seventh. Watching his infant daughter as she lay in her cradle, William Lightfoot felt the same rush of warmth and light he experienced out on the hill when coming up out of a mine into the brilliant sunshine.

"Looking at a baby makes you stop and take stock of things," he said, coming to sit beside Grace, confined to bedrest while regaining her strength. It was early morning. Mary Jeffries would come in soon to stay with Grace for part of the day.

"Babies look so wise. Those wonderful, all-knowing eyes," he said, going back to stand over the tiny bundle again before leaving for the office. "Look at her—she's trying to tell us something. I wonder what babies think about, Grace?"

"I don't know, William. I've often wondered about that too."

"Well, this baby has something to say, and I'd like to know what it is."

William continued to look down at the infant, unaware that it would be thirty years before his younger daughter would present her message to those who chose to hear, and that circumstances and events would not permit him to be among her listeners. He turned then to go to his work, happy in his lot as husband, father, and property surveyor in the gold mining town of Cripple Creek.

All eyes looked westward now to Colorado. Coloradoans proudly went along with the nation's consensus that there was more of everything in Colorado than anywhere else. Discovery of gold in Cripple Creek had helped put the country back on its feet after the panic of 1893, and a grateful America hailed the western stronghold as leader of the country.

In Denver a week-long *Festival of Mountain and Plain* was staged by citizens to celebrate the easing of the depression and the return of prosperity.

In Cripple Creek, encouraged by the upswing in the nation's economy, the Lightfoots and the Jeffrieses decided the time had come for them to return to their former way of life. They planned to move to Denver, where Frank Jeffries would join an engineering firm and William would take a night course in preparation for a position offered by the United States Geological Survey.

Nostalgia gripped them as they packed their possessions. Cripple Creek had been home to them for seven eventful years. They would miss Cripple.

Sitting together before the fire on their last evening in their home on May Street in Cripple Creek, Grace reminded

William that had he not refused Bill Shemwell's Elkton mine offer during their early days in Cripple, the circumstances of their leaving might have been very different and the sum of their accumulated savings much greater. William's reply to his wife's statement of regret was that were he to leave Cripple with no more than he had when he came—the family he loved and who loved him—he would still consider himself very rich.

CHAPTER III

TO BE TOGETHER

"A move's as good as a fire! I don't mind it a bit," Grace Lightfoot told her husband when he remarked on the inconvenience caused by the moving from one location to another required by his work for the United States Geological Survey.

"I never dreamed I'd see so much of the country when I married an engineer. Moving keeps me uncluttered, William. I get rid of all sorts of things simply because I can't be bothered with packing them and taking them along."

"But it's hard on Fairy and Grace Eleanor, I'm afraid —being so young and going from school to school."

"They're bright children, William. And they adjust well. It is hard for them to leave their friends, of course, and to have to make new ones. But in the long run it will have been good experience for them. They'll know how to make themselves at home wherever they go in life. The important thing is for them to be as near to their father as possible, always. The important thing is for all of us to be together."

William's work with the Geological Survey involved resurveying the boundaries of the western states. Since their move to Denver from Cripple Creek, he had been relocated twice by the Department of the Interior, coming off one completed project to be assigned immediately to another.

14

The engineers who made up the surveying corps lived in government camps whose regulations excluded women and children from the premises. Therefore William always traveled alone to a new location, found a house for his family as near to the camp as possible, then sent for them.

He had just been assigned to the surveying of the state lines bordering Kansas. It was a welcome prospect because Grace and the children could live in Manhattan not far from Henry and Eleanor Strong in Bluemont. William would join them weekends as often as possible.

Years later, the Lightfoots looked back on that twelve-month stay in Kansas as their happiest assignment. There were frequent visits to the Strong farm for Sunday dinners, birthdays, and holidays. But inevitably William brought home news of a transfer. They said reluctant good-byes then to the Strongs and their friends and went on to Ogden, Utah, where William worked on the engineering of the railroad from Ogden to Pocatello, Idaho.

William's next commitment took them to Montrose, Colorado. There he joined the crew assigned to the engineering of the Gunnison Tunnel.

It was in Montrose in the second grade of the Central Morgan School that Grace Eleanor formed her memorable association with Miss Kathleen Quinlan. It began at the close of an ordinary school day. Grace Eleanor cleared her desk along with the other children and sat waiting for the dismissal bell. Suddenly, her ears seemed to play a trick on her. Yet there stood her teacher looking directly at her and there was no mistaking her words.

"Grace Eleanor," Miss Quinlan said, "will you stay after school today to read for me, please?"

She could not answer. Her lips felt frozen and there was a lump in her throat. She nodded numbly. Surely there must be some mistake. *She always read her lessons perfectly and had never had to stay after school!* Yet she dared not question her teacher. *It was her birthday, and she had to stay after school to read!*

Miss Quinlan closed the door behind the last child. Grace Eleanor read the lesson, then looked at her teacher. "Miss Quinlan—my mother will think I didn't do well in school today," she said.

"Oh? Oh, well now, we *can't have that.* Let me see. It really isn't too far out of the way—I'll walk along home with you and tell your mother how well you are doing in school. Oh! And today is your *birthday*—your *eighth birthday!*"

It was a beautiful May afternoon. The sun seemed to shine with a special sparkle as they walked together down Cascade Avenue. They turned the corner onto Grace Eleanor's street and Miss Quinlan asked, "Grace Eleanor, is your father home for your birthday?"

"No. He won't be able to come until the end of the month. But I'll have a letter from him today, I know."

They were at her home now and Grace Eleanor led Miss Quinlan through the gate, up the path and onto the porch. She opened the front door to be greeted by a loud "SUR-PRISE!" Stunned, she stood surrounded by her classmates from Central Morgan School. She looked at her mother and Fairy, then turned to Miss Quinlan with happy eyes.

Miss Quinlan wasn't the least bit surprised.

It was early in the school day three weeks later when Miss Quinlan, observing that Grace Eleanor was ill, sent her home from school with a classmate.

"She's sick, Mrs. Lightfoot," Margaret Harding said, holding the door open for Grace Eleanor, then following her into the kitchen.

Grace Lightfoot helped her child into a chair and smoothed her moist forehead.

"Grace Eleanor was sick day before yesterday, too, Mrs. Lightfoot. She's been getting sick a lot lately."

"She's just not up to par right now, that's all. I'm going to have Doctor Hassenplug come over to see her today. Thank you for bringing Grace Eleanor home, Margaret. You're a good friend. Please come back again."

It was evening when Doctor Hassenplug came by. He examined Grace Eleanor as she lay weakly against the pillows.

"This is catarrhal jaundice, Mrs. Lightfoot," he said. "It explains the headaches, fevers, and muscle aches she's been having. As long as the symptoms persist she'll need bed rest. Probably six to eight weeks. I know that's mean of old Doc Hassenplug, Grace Eleanor," he said, bending to give her long curls a tug. "But, if you do everything I say, I'll try to let you up sooner."

"This has been her worst year, Dr. Hassenplug—one thing after another every few weeks, keeping her down for days. And now this."

"I know. In this case, though, bed rest and quiet are important. She's going to be fine. But see that she doesn't take cold. Her susceptibility to colds presents a problem. There's the risk of pneumonia.

"I'm going to prescribe a liver extract. I'll drop in once a week to see how she's coming along. These pills are for migraine," he said, filling a small white envelope from a vial. "Her tendency to migraine is unfortunate. But basically she's got a good constitution. Let's thank God for that, Mrs. Lightfoot."

In the days that followed, Grace Lightfoot knew fear as her daughter's condition worsened.

Then suddenly the child took a turn for the better. Her confinement continued, however, and Grace Eleanor lay listlessly waiting for the time when she could be up and out again. The books and puzzles surrounding her only made her miss Fairy more as the weeks dragged by. No one could read those stories to her the way Fairy could, and no one could pack as much excitement into putting a puzzle together as Fairy. Fairy was away studying home economics at the Kansas State Agricultural College in Manhattan.

It was late June when Dr. Hassenplug allowed Grace Eleanor to be up and about. The days were sunny and warm as if to welcome her as she went outdoors for longer and longer periods each day. But it was only a matter of weeks until a new illness confined her once more.

"Grace Eleanor, get well and stay well!" Fairy told her younger sister when she came home at the close of the spring semester. "Having to go to church without you is a bore! It's no fun at all!"

To the Lightfoot girls, church was someplace to go, something to do twice on Sundays and again Wednesday evenings. Otherwise, church was *church*. The part Fairy and Grace Eleanor liked about it most was going home. It was very pleasant, walking along in their Sunday best with their mother after service, stopping here and there to greet friends.

The test of endurance was over — the hour in the sanctuary when Pastor Reese's words rose to wall them in, as it were, in an atmosphere now chastising, now comforting; now forgiving, now condemning. It was an hour of abject reckoning ending at last with the strains of the recessional which rose to fill them with grateful relief. At this point of deliverance the two girls always glanced at their mother, who sat erect beside them in the pew. There would be the inevitable glow of peace on her face, causing them to wonder what she possibly could have heard to inspire it.

Outside the church one Sunday morning the expression on their mother's face changed abruptly. The set of her lips and the lift to her chin told them that their mother was not pleased. Nor did she linger to greet friends. Placing a hand under each girl's arm, she whisked her daughters out of the churchyard and down the street toward home.

Inside the house, Grace Lightfoot voiced her outrage:

"I have never been so ashamed! The very idea of the two of you behaving that way in church. Snickering and giggling through the sermon like that! I will not have it! I simply will not have it! Do you understand? Let that have been the first and last time!"

"But Mama. Pastor Reese is—*funny*! The way he yells and hacks the air with his arms and points his finger at us—why does he have to get so worked up?"

"Grace Eleanor, that will do! Do you hear me? The very idea, talking like that about a man of the cloth—a man of God. It's sinful!"

"Oh, Mama. Gracie's only telling the truth. What Pastor Reese says is bad enough—but the way he says it is worse! How can he stand before all those people and butcher the English language the way he does? Mixed in with all that doomsday and damnation, it's *hard on the ears*! If he's going to give us hell every Sunday at least he should be grammatical about it!"

"Fairy! Not another word! Do you hear me? *Not another word!* Now go to your rooms and stay there until time for evening service. *Both of you!"*

CHAPTER IV

A DREAM FORFEITED

When they first saw each other Dr. Charles Warren Patch was sitting on the front porch of his home in Concord, New Hampshire, watching an April sunset and Grace Eleanor Lightfoot was putting away her books at the close of school in her eighth grade classroom in Manhattan, Kansas.

It was early evening when Dr. Patch, recuperating from bronchial pneumonia, walked out onto the porch and settled comfortably on the chain-suspended swing. He was in his fifth week of leave from Harvard's School of Dentistry where he taught crown and bridge and he was impatient to get back to work.

As the sun bowed out in a pageant of color Charles Patch sat listening to the sounds of the natural world. Bedding-down birds and spring-heralding peepers filled the air with their tones.

Suddenly he saw her. She seemed as far away as the horizon and as near as the beating of his heart. She moved toward him — this girl he would one day marry — smiling in recognition. The vision faded; then she was gone.

He was on his feet instantly, his eyes searching the place where he had seen her. At last he sat down, looking up to see the first star appear in the twilight sky.

"*Now to find you,*" he breathed into the night. "*Now to find you.*"

In Manhattan, Kansas, at three-thirty in the afternoon that same Tuesday, Miss Maggie Clark reminded her eighth grade class that they had fifteen minutes in which to wind up the day's work on the essays they were preparing for the city-wide contest sponsored by the Manhattan Civic Association.

Grace Eleanor Lightfoot completed her notes and rose to return the encyclopedia she had been using to the bookshelf by the window. She slid the book into place, then paused to look out the window. The afternoon sky had lightened to soft blue and a haze of spring sunshine lay over the land.

She saw him then. He was a tall, distinguished-looking man with silver-gray hair and piercing blue eyes that seemed to look straight through to her soul. He moved toward her along the flat stretch of the horizon, an outdoorsman, a freedom-loving man. She knew, somehow, that he was a doctor, a kind and gentle man who was dedicated to helping people; and she knew that she would some day marry this man.

Just as suddenly, he was gone. Miss Clark's voice came through at that moment, sharply insistent:

"Grace Eleanor! Please take your seat immediately! We are waiting. The bell has rung, my dear!"

The experience was forgotten when she arrived home and heard Fairy announce that she had decided to attend summer school.

Confirmation of Fairy's application to Columbia in New York had come in the morning mail. She would graduate from Kansas State Agricultural College in May. In June she would enter Columbia's graduate school to further study Home Economics.

"Fairy, take the summer off and enjoy yourself! It's been school, school, school. I'd like to see you relax now, and start on your master's a little later," Grace Lightfoot told her older daughter. But when June came, Fairy went on to New York to begin her graduate work.

Meanwhile notice had come of William's new assignment which would take him from Denver to Carson City, Nevada. This time his family would not follow him to his post. In April the four of them had made a weekend visit to Cripple Creek to look over the gold-rush town where Grace Eleanor had been born and Fairy had gone to school. While there, Grace capitulated to Cripple's nostalgic charm. They browsed through the town and made their way up Poverty Gulch to look around the mines on the hill. The two girls toured the *Molly Kathleen* and came up from its depths fascinated.

On the return trip to Denver, Grace brought up the subject of summering in Cripple Creek. It would be like an old times' sake vacation. Fairy and Grace Eleanor warmed to the idea immediately and pressed their father for approval.

"It's not a bad idea at that," William conceded. "Actually it would be much better for all of you not to have to follow me all those hundreds of miles. You're due a break in that pattern. And with Fairy up at Columbia, well — yes — I think it might be a good arrangement, Grace."

Later he said, "It's settled then. I'll get in touch with Jim Weiss in Cripple Creek and have him find us a house."

When June came, the Lightfoots were again in residence in the famous old mining town. And in Cripple Creek, Grace Eleanor was to forge life-long friendships.

"Cripple Creek's a honey of a town. You can feel its zip and zing with every breath you take," she thought, walking down Bennett Avenue early one day to pick up some things for her mother at the Welty and Faulkner Grocery.

"Good morning!"

Smiling cordially as he approached her was a handsome young minister, black-clad and wearing a sparkling white clerical collar.

"Good morning," she said.

"May I introduce myself? I'm David Kirby, pastor of the Baptist Church on Second Street."

"How do you do, Pastor Kirby. I'm Grace Eleanor Light-foot."

"How do you do, Miss Lightfoot. You're new in Cripple Creek?"

"Yes. We've moved here for the summer from Denver."

"It's a pleasure to meet you. I'd like to invite you to come to our Baptist services — Wednesday evenings and Sundays."

"Thank you. Thank you very much, Pastor Kirby. We — we're Methodist."

"I see. Fine! Pastor Davis is a good friend of mine. Let me mention, though, that we've just formed a youth Bible Study group at our church open to young people of all denominations. We'd be happy to have you join us Friday evenings from seven to eight-thirty if you can — interesting study and discussion, and just plain good fun and fellowship. They're a great bunch of young folks. I think you'd enjoy it."

"Thank you, Pastor Kirby. Thank you very much. Well, goodbye now."

Thinking about the encounter as she continued down the street, Grace Eleanor was more impressed than interested.

"Bible study indeed! That's all I need," she thought, swinging into Welty and Faulkner's. *"I spend half my time in church now as it is!"*

Just last week she had run upstairs in a fury of resentment, tears stinging her eyes as she sat down to write to Fairy.

"Mama won't let me do *anything*! Cripple Creek is a great little town, but a lot of good that does *me*! My friends are camping out over the weekend, and Mama won't let me go because I'd miss the Sunday services. You'd think that *just for once in my life* —! Fairy, I get so put out with Mama! All I hear is, 'Now Grace Eleanor, you wouldn't want to be camping out on Sunday if the Lord were to suddenly come.' Or, 'We don't play cards. You wouldn't want to be playing cards if the Lord were to come.' Or, 'We don't dance. You wouldn't

want to be at a dance if the Lord were to come.' Or, 'No indeed. No picture shows. You wouldn't want to be at a picture
show if the Lord were to suddenly come.' Why can't we be free
to enjoy life without the dread of doomsday always hanging
over our heads? And all those creepy predictions of the end
of the world! Oh, I wish we weren't Methodists. Other people
— the Catholics and the Episcopalians, for instance — *have lots
more fun!*"

In New York, Fairy too was feeling the need for more
varied expression. Halfway through the summer session at
Columbia, she decided she wanted to put her Home Economics training into practice. Fairy made up her mind then to
find a teaching job beginning with the school term in September. She would teach, but where? New York? Denver? Walking down to the student post office to check the morning
mail, Fairy was still mulling the question of place. A letter
lay in her box addressed in her mother's familiar hand. She
went to her room and opened the letter, standing by the window as she read: "We are going to stay in Cripple Creek. Your
father has written that he will be working in Carson City until
next spring or early summer, and he wants us to stay put.

"Grace Eleanor will go to Cripple Creek High in September. She's tickled pink. She loves it here."

Fairy read the remainder of the letter and laid it on her
desk. Then she picked it up and read it again.

*"Grace Eleanor will go to Cripple Creek High in Septem-
ber. She's tickled pink. She loves it here."*

She refolded the letter and returned it to its envelope. Sitting on the edge of her desk, she looked about her dorm
room.

*Cripple Creek. Why not? It's got atmosphere and I like
that. I've got to teach somewhere. It's as good a place as any.
I'm going to apply for a job at Cripple Creek High School.*

Acknowledgement of her inquiry came within a week. There was an opening in Home Economics in Cripple Creek High School. Within three weeks Fairy's application was processed and an interview date set for August twenty-seventh, six days after the close of the Columbia summer session. She wrote home about her plans.

"We had no idea you were considering such a thing," her mother wrote back. "This is wonderful! Your father will be so pleased. And Grace Eleanor is thrilled."

Coming home to Cripple Creek, Fairy found her sister a popular member of Cripple's younger set. And she found her still railing against the same restrictions.

At dinner on Fairy's third day at home, Grace Eleanor mentioned that her friends were meeting at Mabel Nickols' home that evening for cards. When she asked for permission to go, her mother refused.

Leaving her meal unfinished, Grace Eleanor pushed back her chair and ran upstairs to her bedroom. "Now look here, Mama," Fairy began.

"Please stay out of it, Fairy. She's not going to play cards. Cards are a contrivance of the devil."

"No, I'm not going to stay out of it, Mama! I'm not going to stand by and watch you hold Gracie down the way you held me down! You've got to loosen up a little where Gracie is concerned — give her more freedom. You must let her play cards and learn to dance — let her be social and active. It's only right that she should *go places* and *do things*! Now, at last, I've come into a feeling of freedom myself, and I want Gracie to have that freedom, too. And for heaven's sake stop calling her *Grace Eleanor*. It makes her cringe in front of her friends. Call her *Gracie*. Everybody else does. Even Papa calls her *Gracie*."

Life became happier for Gracie with Fairy at home. She marvelled at Fairy's influence with her mother. She was proud of Fairy. Until her sister became a teacher, Gracie had always thought of teachers as a special breed from some far-off world, authoritative beings unlike ordinary humans, poker-faced and oppressive in their power to dictate, direct, and demand—with the exception of Miss Kathleen Quinlan in Montrose, Colorado.

But now to fifteen-year-old Gracie and her friends at Cripple Creek High, the beautiful, fashionable Fairy represented a welcome change in the traditional school-teacher image. Gracie was proud of Fairy's rapport with the students. And she was grateful to her. Fairy's influence at home had opened the way to greater freedom, and she loved her for it.

Now, school was in recess for the holiday. It was the day after Thanksgiving and Cripple Creek shivered under a blanket of heavy snow. Cripple's surrounding hills rang with the shouts of youngsters sledding, skiing, and snowballing.

In the white frame house beyond the courthouse on Bennett Avenue William and Grace Lightfoot sat before the fire with their coffee. William had arrived in Cripple Creek Tuesday and would stay with his family until Sunday.

Gracie came in the front door breathless from the cold and William turned to look at her.

"Come sit by the fire and get warm, Gracie."

"First I'll get something hot to drink," she said, pulling off her boots and going to the kitchen.

"She looks wonderful," William remarked to Grace.

"I'm so pleased with her, William. She's been ill only once since we've been here and only for a short time, at that."

Gracie came back with her chocolate and took the chair by her father. Her mother sat with them for awhile then excused herself to start dinner.

William placed another log on the fire. When the flare of sparks had settled, he went back to his chair.

"Papa, what do you think I should do when I get out of

high school? What do you think I should be?" Gracie asked him.

The fresh log, wrapped in flames now, burned briskly. William waited for a few moments, gazing at the fire. Then he said,

"What would you *like* to do, Gracie? What would you *like* to be?"

"I don't know."

"Well, it seems to me that if you can just live in a community and *mean* something to it — be of value wherever you are by doing your very best and giving your very best, why, that would be good. You will find, Gracie, that life has a way of letting us know what it expects of us, what it is that we should do. At the right time it will come to you. Then you'll know."

Gracie couldn't put her finger on just what it was three weeks later that made her decide to visit Pastor Kirby's Youth Bible Study Group. Surprised at the fun the first session held for her, she joined the young people regularly each week thereafter.

Pastor David Kirby was no ordinary teacher. Nor did he take an ordinary approach to the subject matter he presented. The youthful minister established an easy rapport with his young people and to their amazement proceeded to turn the Bible inside out and upside down. Its archaic heroes and heroines came to life in a way that had Abraham, Sarah, Rebekkah, Isaac, Jacob, Rachel, Moses, Samson, David, and Solomon all but standing in flesh and blood reality in their midst. He held these pillars of biblical history up to the light for scrutiny and analysis, and, when called for, pulled the skeletons out of their respective closets.

Kirby's characters were not paragons of virtue *per se* whose superior spiritual powers merited them man's unqualified, worshipful regard; they were, rather, persevering human beings who once lived on earth and were tempted "just as I am, just as you are." At various times and under certain circumstances, he pointed out, these lofty individuals faltered and fell; were capable of sin, disobedience, deception—an overall missing of the mark. Nevertheless, niches of merit were carved out for them in biblical history when, through discipline and obedience at a particular point in their lives, they were lifted to the heights of spiritual enlightenment and inspiration.

Through Pastor David Kirby's comprehensive interpretations, the men and women of the Bible became credible characters representing points of identification for his students that had been inconceivable to them before. They were inclined now to regard the Bible as a purposeful guide; plausible; encouraging to those who through principled living aspire to worthwhile goals. For Gracie, Pastor Kirby's sessions sparked an interest in the Bible that was to keep her studying its pages throughout her entire life.

During her senior year at Cripple Creek High, Gracie approached her studies with an interest that soared in geology class. The course held great appeal for her and Miss Gerald praised her handling of its subject matter.

In late April Miss Gerald led her senior students eastward from town and up Poverty Gulch to gather rock specimens in the vicinity of Globe Hill. Gracie persevered until she had checked off the entire list: Pike's Peak and Cripple Creek granite, agate, quartz, turquoise, feldspar, mica, calcity, sandstone, petrified wood, and fossils. Her collection earned her special credit and a display niche in her mother's china cabinet.

"I could go into this field of work and be very happy," she remarked to her mother as she arranged her specimens inside the glass-fronted case. "It may well be for me."

It was the most exciting year of her life. She was caught up in a whirl of activity—holiday dances, parties, campouts, long walks and talks with close friends atop Mount Pisgah, graduation preparations, the senior prom, and her Saturday night dates. Happy as she was, there persisted the question, *"What shall I do with my life? What shall I be?"*

Finally she had the answer. She knew exactly what it was that she wanted to do, what she wanted to be. She would study medicine. She wanted to be a doctor.

There remained the problem of how to broach the subject to her mother. She was aware that it was not a woman's profession. She would need to ask questions about it.

"Yes, there are a few women doctors, very few. I don't know any," Grace Lightfoot said in answer to her daughter.

"It's not women's work, Gracie. That kind of work is much too hard for a woman. Why?"

"I keep thinking about what I should do, Mother. I'd like to be a doctor — a surgeon. Of all the things to be, nothing could be more rewarding than being responsible for the way people feel after they've been very ill and you've made them well."

"Yes. Well, *you can forget about that right now.* That would never do for you, Gracie. You're not strong enough for that kind of life. The demands, the pressures, the responsibilities would be too much for you, Gracie — as sickly as you've been all your life. Your health would break under the strain."

It had been late June when she first talked with her mother about studying medicine. In spite of her mother's objections, the idea remained fixed in her mind.

"This time you're off course," Fairy told her when Gracie went to her asking for support in convincing their mother. "No, I won't talk to Mama about it. That's out. You couldn't possibly take it. No indeed, Gracie. *Forget it.*"

But Gracie was determined. She wrote to the University of California at Berkeley requesting information about its premed program. A catalog and application form arrived within a week.

Her father was on location in California, working on a highlands project in the coastal ranges along the western edge of the state. She would have her father nearby. It would work out perfectly. Gracie wrote to him of her plans.

She approached her mother again.

Grace Lightfoot remained firm. Gracie would go, she stated flatly, where they'd all gone—to Kansas State Agricultural College in Kansas. And she would take Home Economics, as Fairy had done, and as befitted all sensible young women.

Gracie's last hope lay with her father. It waned when his letter came. He agreed with her mother that it was not the right thing for her to do. He was certain that she would be happy at Kansas State Agricultural College, where he and her mother and Fairy had gone, and where her grandparents' farm was close by.

September with its ultimatum came all too soon for Gracie, putting an end to the good times she shared with her friends. They went their separate ways then, some to college, others to their respective jobs.

Nostalgia gripped Gracie as she boarded the train for Kansas with her mother at Cripple Creek's Midland Terminal. It would take them first to Divide, then to Colorado Springs where they would change to the Colorado Midland Railway for Denver.

At Denver's Union Station they boarded the Union Pacific for Manhattan, a journey of five hundred miles.

Gracie looked out the window at the gorgeous late summer scenery. Snowcaps lay like mantles across the shoulders of her beloved mountains. She would miss the Rockies terribly. She kept her eyes on their great granite peaks, for soon their majestic beauty would lie behind her. They would be approaching the Kansas border and the inevitable leveling of the land.

Night fell. The rhythmic grind of the train's wheels lulled her to sleep as she lay in her berth thinking of all that she had left behind — all that was familiar and dear.

She awoke the next morning and peered out of the window, struggling to cope with the incredible starkness of the Kansas horizon. Against it, endless expanses of ripe wheat rippled in the breeze while here and there huddles of sunflowers lifted their heads to the sun.

They arrived in Manhattan in late afternoon. Grandmother and Grandfather Strong were at the station to meet them when they stepped down from the platform. Her grandmother seemed smaller to Gracie than she had remembered. She moved more slowly now, and held to Grandfather Strong's arm tightly as the four of them walked along.

CHAPTER V

THE FAMILY ALMA MATER

"Gracie! Gracie Lightfoot!"

Gracie stopped in her tracks at the ring of the familiar voice behind her and turned around expectantly.

"Well, Don McCarten! Hello!"

Gracie looked incredulously at the lanky youth from Cripple Creek as he spanned the ground between them grinning happily.

"Well, I'll be darned, Gracie! What are you doing *here*? I thought you wanted to go to Berkeley?"

"*I wanted to*—but my folks didn't see things my way. KSAC is the family alma mater. I'm here on the strength of that."

"I'm glad! What's your major?"

"Home Economics."

"Oh—here working on your MRS., eh?" Don teased her.

"Hm—two weeks of college and you're full of smart remarks. What's yours?"

"Veterinary Medicine."

"Of course—what else. Who's looking after your menagerie while you're here at school?"

"My brother Phil. I brought some of it along—my hamsters and white mice and my African frogs."

"Hey—I bet your roommates like that!"

Gracie and Don had graduated together from Cripple Creek High School. They had traveled in separate crowds, but Gracie often passed the McCarten place on her walks to Mount Pisgah, and always stopped to talk with Don over the fence and to watch him at work with his animals. Many times she had over-ridden Don's good-natured objections and coaxed a favorite flop-eared burro into following her to Pisgah, luring him along with thistle-flowers and returning him to Don on the way home.

Don walked with Gracie to her next class.

"There's a class meeting in the auditorium Thursday at two-thirty," he told her. "Meet me in the concourse at two-fifteen and we'll go together."

"Okay. I'll be there," Gracie said, leaving Don at the door of her English class.

During a later class meeting nominations for class officers were held and Don nominated Gracie for class treasurer. The gregarious McCarten campaigned for his candidate vigorously, promoting her as "KSAC's Girl From the World's Greatest Gold Camp, Cripple Creek, Colorado."

Gracie won by a landslide.

Her duties as freshman class treasurer involved her in many activities, and Don McCarten became a frequent escort. The sight of Don's tall, lanky figure loping into view always cheered Gracie. His friendship had taken the edge off the newness of her environment, and she was grateful for his presence.

Her days at KSAC grew increasingly pleasant. By spring she had grown fond of the college and was happy there.

At the close of the spring semester she and Don McCarten boarded the *Pacific Coast Limited* together one evening to return to Cripple Creek for the summer. They were well into Colorado the next morning when the conductor announced an emergency stop-over in Limon for repairs.

Following inspection of the affected car, a further delay of forty minutes was called. Passengers were free to disboard for thirty minutes, the conductor told them.

Don reached to help Gracie as she stepped down from the platform. They walked along the tracks and looked around. Gracie saw some wildflowers across the field. There was enough time. She wanted to pick some. They walked quickly to the spot and found clumps of wild daisies, iris, spreads of purple sage and blue alfalfa. Gracie and Don looked up to see a slender white-tail doe feeding in an open clearing. The two of them stood very still, watching her. Lifting her head, the doe looked about with her huge velvety eyes, her snowy throat and tawny torso glistening in the morning sunlight.

The harsh bang of clanging metal shattered the air and in one lightning-swift bolt the deer vanished. Gracie looked at Don regretfully.

Realization struck them both in that instant and they broke into a run. Gracie and Don approached the moving train, waving and shouting frantically. They were too late. The train continued steadily down the tracks, leaving them stranded alongside. The pair stared after it, stunned and disbelieving. *Their train had left without them!*

"*Don! Don, what are we going to do?*" Gracie's tone was desperate.

"Gracie, I—don't know." Don's gaze faltered and he looked away from Gracie. He turned then, shoved his hands in his pockets and kicked at a slab of granite.

"Don, *what are we going to do? Oh! My family will have a fit! Especially Mama!*"

"I'll tell you what we're going to do, Gracie. We're going to go into Limon and get ourselves out of this. Right now. Come on. Let's go."

In Limon Gracie telephoned home. There was no answer. Her mother was on her way to Denver, of course, to meet her train—due in Union Station at twelve noon.

They asked about the cost of a hired car. Between them they did not have enough money to cover it.

They walked to the train station, and Don kept a reassuring arm around Gracie's shoulder. Inside the Limon Station Don explained their predicament to the stationmaster. He offered to put them on the next train to Denver. Local No. 101 would leave Limon at one-forty-five that afternoon, he told them. It would arrive in Denver at five o'clock.

At Denver's Union Station, Grace Lightfoot relaxed with a book and waited for her daughter's train. According to the timetable it would be arriving an hour and ten minutes late.

When the *Pacific Coast Limited* pulled into the station and Gracie was not among those who got off, Grace Lightfoot went to check with the conductor to see if all passengers had disboarded. He investigated, then returned to assure her that they had. She went to the desk and talked with the station agent. Then she telephoned the college in Kansas. Gracie had signed out at six o'clock the evening before, they told her. Her listed destination was Cripple Creek, Colorado.

Grace hung the telephone on its hook, struggling with a growing sense of fear. *What had happened to Gracie? Where was she?*

She telephoned Fairy. Fairy had married recently, and she and her husband, Fred Strout, a widower with three children, had moved to their new home on High Street in Denver only a week ago. Grace was grateful for their nearness now.

Perhaps she had met the wrong train, Fairy suggested. But Grace Lightfoot had her younger daughter's letter with her in her purse. *The Pacific Coast Limited, Tuesday, May twenty-ninth at twelve o'clock noon.*

Grace waited while Fairy told Fred the situation.

She was not to worry, Fairy told her mother. Fred would come to the station to pick her up right away. Then he would go back to meet the incoming trains.

Local No. 101 ground to a halt once more thirty-eight miles outside of Limon. There was the problem now of overheated journal bearings. There would be a delay, the conductor advised, until a car mechanic could be summoned from the Limon Station.

It was pitch dark when Gracie and Don arrived at Denver's Union Station.

"*Why*, Gracie, *why?*" her brother-in-law greeted her icily, his face a censuring mask. Gracie was stunned by the harshness of Fred's manner.

"*Why would you do a thing like this?*" he persisted, anger smoldering in his eyes. "*Do you know what you've put your mother through? Why? Why?*"

He ignored Gracie's explanation, and acknowledged the introduction to Don McCarten coldly.

"Where is your luggage?" he demanded.

Although Gracie's luggage had been ticketed for Denver, they found when they checked with the baggage clerk that it had been mistakenly sent to Colorado Springs. Don offered to pick it up for her along with his own on his way to Cripple Creek. As Don prepared to leave, Fred Strout turned to light his pipe, pointedly avoiding the exchange of goodnights. Don took the hand Gracie held out to him.

"*You're pure gold, Gracie,*" he said softly, "*real Cripple Creek gold.*"

Home at last, Gracie bore her mother's reprimands patiently. How could she be so thoughtless? Why had she not let them know about the delay? Gracie's response that she had phoned but received no answer went unheeded.

"And have you begun to research our genealogy as I asked you to do? *No.* It's the least you could have done for me, Gracie. You've been at college one year, with a library to use and professors to guide you. I've asked you a dozen times. "Well—out of sight, out of mind," Grace Lightfoot fumed.

"I'm sorry, Mama. I just haven't gotten to it, somehow. After spring vacation I'll get right on it."

"It'll *never* get done! I went through the same thing with

you, Fairy," Grace added, giving her older daughter a censuring look.

"Oh, Mama," Fairy soothed, "why are you so concerned
about your genealogy? What if your ancestry does date back
to the Revolutionary War? Family trees are the bunk! You've
got me and Gracie and Papa and Grandmother and Grandfather Strong to keep you busy here and now. And Fred and
the three youngsters make four more besides!"

Grace Lightfoot walked across the kitchen to the pantry
and hung her apron behind the door.

"You know, Mama," Fairy went on, "someone once said,
'It's fine to be well-descended, but the glory belongs to our
ancestors!' And somebody else said, 'The person who boasts
of his ancestors is admitting he's better dead than alive!' "

Their mother put the cream away with a firm close of the
icebox door and walked out of the kitchen in a frosty silence.

Sitting at the table with their coffee, the two sisters looked
at each other.

"One of us should have looked into it for her, really," Fairy
admitted.

"I'll do it, Fairy. But for the life of me I can't get excited
about 'way back then!' Now—this minute—and us—is what's
important to me!"

Gracie began an investigation of the Lightfoot lineage as
soon as she returned to college in late March. She started by
browsing in the reference room of the KSAC library. Going
at it alphabetically, she looked up "Lightfoot," then "Strong."
Seated at a study table with her resource materials before her,
she combed the pages of a heavy volume and came upon a
picture of an austere-looking gentleman who gazed at her
with beneficent eyes. He was Bishop Lightfoot of the Church
of England. Gracie studied his features carefully to see if she
could note a resemblance between him and her father. There
was none.

About to turn the page and go on, she stopped suddenly. She could not be sure if she had heard it or felt it or both.

"Someday you, too, will be in the clergy," was the substance of the message. *"You, too, will become a minister."*

As the words echoed in her mind, Gracie peered at the bishop's picture closely. She shrugged off the experience then and turned the page. Its impact faded and with time she forgot about it.

Gracie's attempt to gather genealogical data for her mother proved futile. But before abandoning the project she discussed it with one of her professors, who suggested she investigate the archives in Washington, D.C.

Explaining to her mother that she had done all she could, Gracie gave her attention to the activities going on at KSAC, whose pulse center was lively Anderson Hall. Anderson Hall ran the length of the Kansas State Agricultural College's instructional building. The campus Post Office was located mid-point on the first floor. Each morning at eleven-twenty Gracie hurried from her upper-level third period class and made her way among the milling students to check her mailbox. Then she walked to the opposite end of the hall.

It was spring and the sun this Tuesday morning streamed through the window at the foot of the stairs, reflecting from the walls and lighting up a poster displayed beside the last office on the right.

Gracie stopped to scan the poster's message. She moved closer then and read it in detail. She must have those words. She wanted them with her, to read again and again. After her last class that afternoon, she returned to copy them.

"There is nothing I can give you which you have not; but there is much, very much that while I cannot give it, you can take. No heaven can come to us unless our hearts find rest in today. Take Heaven! No peace lies in the future which is not hidden in this present instant. Take Peace!

". . . . . Life is a generous giver, but we, judging its gifts by their covering, cast them aside as ugly, or heavy, or hard. Remove the covering, you will find beneath it, a living splendor, woven of love, by wisdom, with power. Welcome it, grasp it, and you touch the angel's hand that brings it to you. Everything we call a trial, a sorrow, or a duty, believe me, that angel's hand is there; the gift is there, and the wonder of an overshadowing Presence. . . . ."

—Fra Giovanni
1513, A. D.

Gracie made a point of looking at the poster each morning. She noted that its contents changed every other day. At the end of the day she would copy writings that held particular meaning for her:

"Let your mind be quiet, realizing the beauty of the world, and the immense, the boundless treasures that it holds in store.

"All that you have within you, all that your heart desires, all that your nature so specially fits you for—that or the counterpart of it waits embedded in the great Whole, for you. It will surely come to you.

"Yet equally sure not one moment before its appointed time will it come. . . ."

—Edward Carpenter
*The Lake of
Beauty*

As Gracie stood writing one Friday afternoon the door to the office opened and a woman in physician's attire stepped out, a stethoscope dangling about her neck and a sheaf of papers over her arm. Gracie moved aside quickly and closed her notebook.

"It's all right," the woman smiled. "Go right ahead."

"Thank you. I was just copying something from this poster."

"Are you interested in what's there?"

"Yes, I certainly am."

"Good."

"Are you the one who puts these things here?"

"Yes."

"Oh, they're marvelous. Where do you get them?"

"You'd really like to know?"

"Indeed I would."

"Well now, you can come to my office Monday evenings and find out. I meet with a study group here Mondays at seven-thirty. The students use several books and periodicals that contain these thoughts and ideas. You are welcome to join us if you wish."

"Thank you. I'd like to come."

Dr. Mary Parker was diminutive and blue-eyed with brown hair and a warm and gracious manner. Thirty-five students crowded her office Monday evenings to study Frank Channing Haddock's "The Power of the Will." Take-out literature was available to the students. Gracie became interested in a metaphysical journal called "The Nautilus," edited monthly in Boston by Elizabeth Towne.

In Dr. Parker's office Gracie began to find answers to some of the questions she had asked all her life, questions whose answers had been, *"That's just the way things are, Gracie. Accept them." "We weren't meant to understand these things." "It is the will of God; you must not question it." "It was not intended that we should understand the mystery of life while on earth. After we pass on, we will know. It will all be revealed to us then."*

Dr. Parker presented something she referred to as Principle — Universal Principle — unity in the trinity of man, mind and the universe; unity in the trinity of science, philosophy, and religion. It made sense. It was intelligent. It was comfortable.

Gracie gained immeasurably from Dr. Parker's meetings and attended them regularly throughout her stay at the Kansas State Agricultural College.

CHAPTER VI

TURNING POINT

The evening of Gracie's eighteenth birthday, May seventh, 1915, news of the sinking of the unarmed passenger liner *The Lusitania* reached the Lightfoots in Cripple Creek. William had been on location in California and Grace at home with Gracie when word came of the day's tragedy which claimed the lives of one-hundred-twenty-four Americans along with a thousand others.

Thousands of Americans demanded retaliation. But President Wilson held to a course of restraint, persisting with infinite patience in his attempts at peaceful negotiations.

"HE KEPT US OUT OF WAR" was the slogan that won Wilson re-election in 1916. He had made valiant efforts to end the war by active mediation. He had worked tirelessly to preserve the peace. His was a grateful people.

But the subsequent launching of unrestricted submarine warfare by the Germans against all vessels found in zones off the Allied coasts, neutrals included, constituted a breach of international law. Although his desire was for peace, President Wilson was left with no alternative but to ask Congress for a declaration of war.

Congress declared war on April 6, 1917.

Along with the rest of the country, the little mining town of Cripple Creek, Colorado, rallied to the cause to a man.

War was no stranger to Cripple Creek. In 1903 at the peak

of her boom, the entire district had been terrorized by the ruthless hostilities of a labor war which resulted in thirty-five deaths and the ultimate collapse of organized labor in the renowned gold camp. Declared by the Western Federation of Miners, a strike idled nearly four-thousand men and precipitated Cripple's decline in production and population after the turn of the century.

Cripple Creek never rallied from the blow. A mass exodus took place as thousands began moving out of the district. Cripple Creek, once Colorado's third largest city, dwindled to a community of five thousand, made up mostly of workers employed by powerful corporation bosses.

And now—spring, 1918—the World War, which ultimately would close the remaining one hundred fifty ore-shipping mines, cast a further lull over the gold camp.

The times reflected worldwide upheaval, change, and adjustment. Grace Lightfoot coped with these in her own life, shaken first by the sudden death of her mother in late autumn, then only months later by the death of her father.

With Gracie away at college, coming home only for holidays, Grace lived winters in Denver now in an apartment not far from Fairy's and Fred's home on High Street. William continued in an extended assignment on the west coast and he, too, came home only for holidays. They had kept their house in Cripple Creek, however, so that Grace and Gracie could spend summers there.

When Gracie returned to Cripple Creek with her mother in May 1918, only Cecelia Braden of the old crowd was on hand to meet her. Most of the girls had gone into nurses' training, and the young men were away serving in the armed forces or manning defense jobs. The good times and get-togethers of other years were just a memory now. Gracie herself had enrolled at the University of Colorado for summer study and would leave Cripple Creek for Boulder the second week of June. It had been while she was at home in Denver for Christmas that Gracie told her parents of her intent to change courses and schools. She still wanted to study medicine, she had asserted. It was a must with her.

"I've gone as far as I can go in Home Economics," Gracie said. "These three years at KSAC were all right. They were practically all science courses. But I'm not interested in becoming a Home Economics teacher—or in entering the Home Economics field—so there's no point in wasting the coming year. I've made up my mind. This is what I want to do."

Grace Lightfoot's eyes met her husband's.

"William—she hasn't the slightest idea what she'll be in for! She's not built to take that sort of thing—she hasn't the strength for that kind of life!"

"Oh, for heaven's sake, Mama. I'm strong enough," Gracie objected. "I'll be all right. You'll see." She excused herself then and went to her room.

"*Now what*, William? She's back on that subject again," Grace fretted.

"She's a young woman now, Grace, with a mind of her own."

"It'll be too much for her, William!"

"Now, now, Grace. I'm sure that long before Gracie starts carrying a little black bag she'll be thinking about using her Home Economics training to make her husband comfortable and happy."

"Well, *I hope so,* William. *I certainly hope so.*"

By mid-July 1918, Gracie Lightfoot had been involved in the pre-med curriculum at the University of Colorado in Boulder for more than a month.

Although the reality of a world hopelessly enmeshed in war hung over the earth, the sun shone down peacefully on the University of Colorado, structured in stately dignity along the southern edge of Boulder. Everything about it was beautiful. Its buildings were rural Italian, their red-tiled roofs rising and sloping at varying heights and angles. Boulder Creek came tumbling down the mountainside past the university campus. To the north on University Lake, water lilies floated in chaste perfection.

Passing Macky Auditorium on her way to Old Main, Gracie hugged the scene to her. It was good to be here. Two of her closest high school friends, Harriet Shaw and Mabel Nickols, were students in the University's school of nursing. She planned to look them up after her last class Friday.

Friday's attempt to visit her friends failed, however. A second try Monday proved unsuccessful.

"Miss Shaw has night duty this week and is resting now. Miss Nickols is on duty at this time until three o'clock," the receptionist explained to Gracie.

"I see. Would it be possible to see Miss Nickols after three then?"

"I believe she has a class at three. Let me check," the receptionist said, looking through her schedule book once more. "Yes. Miss Nickols will be in class until five o'clock. You may call at five, if you wish."

And with five o'clock success came at last.

"Gracie Lightfoot, it's been ages since I've seen you!" Mabel Nickols exclaimed, coming down the hallway toward her friend.

"Oh, I know!"

"Come on—let's go outside. I've been cooped up in here all day!"

"It's almost dinnertime, Mabel. Let's go out to eat somewhere so we can talk."

"I'd like that. But I can't, Gracie. We have to eat in the dining room. I've only half-an-hour right now."

They walked across the lawn and sat down on a bench.

"Mabel, I've been looking for you and Harriet ever since I got here. Where in the world do you keep yourselves?"

"I knew you were here, Gracie. Cecelia wrote us about it. We just haven't had a chance to look you up. Our schedules are really tight, Gracie. I hardly ever see Harriet. Well, how do you like UC, and what are you taking?"

"*I love it!* I'm taking Anatomy and Biochemistry right now. How about you?"

"I just came out of Medical-Surgical Nursing. Gracie, are you still going with Walter?"

"Yes. He'll be here Saturday. He's at the University of Denver in engineering. We're going to the Variety Show at Macky Auditorium Saturday night. Could we all meet and go together?"

"I'll be on duty then, Gracie. I don't know about Harriet. I think she'll be getting ready to go on night duty at ten."

"For heaven's sake, Mabel. Don't you ever get a break? You're not having any fun!"

"Neither are our patients. It's the war, Gracie. There just aren't enough nurses. It's a desperate situation—there's more work than hands to do it."

Mabel glanced at her watch.

"Gosh—I hate to rush off, Gracie, but I've got to get back. Listen—I'm off Sunday—my first Sunday off in three weeks! Come over at one o'clock and we'll walk into town."

"Okay."

"I'll tell Harriet you were here. So long. See you Sunday."

Early Sunday afternoon, Walter Pennock waited on the University of Colorado Hospital lawn while Grace hurried up the steps and disappeared inside to call for Mabel and Harriet.

"Miss Lightfoot, there's a message for you here from Miss Nickols. She's been called into emergency surgery. She'll get in touch with you soon," the receptionist at the desk told Gracie.

"I see. Can you tell me if Miss Shaw is free at this time, please?"

"I'll check. No, Miss Shaw is resting now. She came off night duty this morning."

"Thank you very much."

Gracie walked across the lobby toward the door. On the right was a huge poster propped on the floor at an eye-catching angle. It pictured a young woman in civilian clothes observing a wounded soldier being helped by a uniformed nurse. "WE NEED YOU" the print stated boldly. Gracie studied the poster, then went out the door and down to the lawn where Walter Pennock stood waiting.

"Walt, they're both tied up and can't come after all," Gracie told him, her face mirroring her disappointment.

"Aw, shucks. That is too bad. Now I have you all to myself," Walter teased. He put an arm around Gracie's shoulder and they walked off together into the warm afternoon.

They wandered down the main streets of Boulder, mingling with Sunday strollers and peering into shop windows; the good looking, sandy-haired youth, tall, handsomely dressed in a brown blazer and beige flannels, and the lovely young girl, stunning in a rose-pink suit and white waistcoat, the sun accenting the sheen of her black hair.

Placards were on display everywhere, alerting the public to the "SAVING MEANS VICTORY" program practiced all over the country. Slogans lined storefronts: "VICTORY LIBERTY LOAN—FOR HOME AND COUNTRY"; "OBSERVE MEATLESS, WHEATLESS, AND GASLESS DAYS"; "AMERICA'S WAR INDUSTRIES NEED YOUR JUNK"; "UNCLE SAM NEEDS THAT EXTRA SHOVELFUL OF COAL."

At the post office a poster read: "NURSES WANTED. 25,000 STUDENT NURSES. U.S. STUDENT NURSE RESERVE."

Further along at the Municipal Building, a Red Cross communique showed a wounded soldier attended by two nurses. "IF I FAIL HE DIES," its caption read.

The pair had dinner in a downtown restaurant, then ambled through Chautauqua Park until dusk. Her hand in Walt's as they walked toward the exit, Gracie was silent, thoughtful.

They continued along for some time, then Walt said,

"Okay, Gracie. Let's have it. Something's on your mind."

"Walt—I'm glad you were here with me today. I've come to an important decision."

"We'll get married before graduation?"

"Oh, Walt—be serious!"

"I am serious, Gracie."

"I know, Walt. But we said we would wait. We agreed to wait until—Walt, you'll be going into the service soon. How in the world would we manage? But let's not talk about that now."

Gracie stopped and took both Walt's hands in hers. She looked at him intently.

"Walt, I'm going to go into nursing."

"You want to be a nurse? You want to go into nurses' training?"

"Yes."

"When?"

"Now. I'm going to look into it right away. Tomorrow."

Walt was silent for a time. Then he said,

"Hm. Well, it's okay, Gracie, if that's what you want to do. It's right up your alley, all right. I guess it's okay with your folks, hm?"

"It won't be okay with Mama. So I'm not going to say anything about it. I'm just—going to *go ahead and do it*. Walt, I want to help. There's a tremendous need. *I have to help!* I won't be able to stand it if I don't. But I have to know that you understand, Walt—that you think it's right," Gracie said.

"I love you, Gracie. I want you to do whatever makes you happy," he told her. "So it's all right with old Walt here. Yes. I think it's a good thing."

In the office of the dean of nurses later that month Gracie sat erect in a chair across from the interviewing dean.

"You have a strong background in science, Miss Lightfoot," the dean remarked. "This is fine. Nurses are a very special breed indeed — at once scientists and humanitarians. I believe you are well qualified for the work.

"Your application, transcripts, and references have been approved by our staff. At the close of this interview, you are to report to Miss Anderson's office. She will assign you a duty and class schedule. Bacteriology and Nursing Arts will be your beginning subjects. And, oh yes," she added, picking up a long white envelope, "take this letter to the listed address and arrange for the fitting and purchase of your uniforms."

Mrs. Kearns extended her hand to Gracie. "It's a pleasure to welcome you into our profession, my dear. Good luck to you."

The weeks and months that followed were crammed with study, class attendance, and duty assignments. The hospital's training regimen demanded total commitment, involvement that left little time for the outside world. Except for occasional correspondence with her parents and sister, and weekly letters to Walt, Gracie's thoughts seldom went beyond her immediate duties and responsibilities. The work pace was often overwhelming. But Gracie loved it. She loved everything about it.

One day during her fourth month of training, Gracie came off duty and went downstairs to answer a call from the main desk.

"There's a message for you, Miss Lightfoot. Mr. Walter Pennock called for you. He's waiting on the south lawn and would like to see you before you go to dinner."

"Thank you, Mrs. Martinelli."

Gracie walked across the lobby to the entrance. She stood looking about for a moment, then hurried down to the lawn where Walter was waiting.

"Walt! Didn't you get my letter? I—had to work today. One of the girls in our unit is ill."

"I got your letter, Gracie."

"Then—why did you—"

"I wanted to see you."

"But—I've only half an hour right now!"

"Well, then you have only half an hour."

"But Walt! You came all the way up here—"

"To see you. For half an hour. That's right."

She looked at him incredulously.

"I miss you, Gracie. It's been almost two months since I've seen you."

"I'm glad you came, Walt. I've missed you too. A lot."

Her hands were in his now.

"You're really happy here," Walt said then.

"Yes. I love it here. I love everything about it. Oh, Walt—being in love with you—and my work here—I never dreamed life could be so perfect!"

"I had dinner with Fairy and Fred last week. Your mother is doing Red Cross volunteer work. They think you've inspired her."

Recalling her mother's reaction when she'd entered nurses' training, they laughed. They walked along slowly hand in hand until they came to a bench beneath a shade tree. They sat and talked for a time, then were silent. Just being together was enough.

Aware that the time was passing quickly, Gracie glanced at her watch.

"Walt—I'm sorry. I've got to go in now."

They walked across the lawn to the hospital entrance.

"I'll see you next Sunday, Gracie," Walt told her.

"Walt—I—forfeited my Sunday off. It will be three weeks until—"

"I know. You told me in your letter. But I'll see you next Sunday, same time. Right here."

"But I'll only have half an hour again! Walt—you *mustn't*—it's *too expensive*—"

"Next Sunday. I'll be waiting."

Their times together were precious and few. On an August afternoon they picnicked in Chautauqua Park and when the golden sun of summer burned into autumn they climbed Flagstaff Mountain to look out on the world below, standing ankle-deep in leaves and listening to the calls of birds echoing along canyon walls. In a late October snow they bundled in parkas and toboganned on the hillsides with Fred Shepherd, Mabel Nickols, Harriet Shaw and Clarence Smith, warming themselves around a bonfire under a moonlit sky. On the eleventh day of November they rejoiced with a war-weary world that danced and paraded ecstatically in the streets, celebrating the signing of the armistice that marked the end of international conflict and the long awaited return of peace.

The war over, the path ahead for Gracie and Walt lay smooth and tranquil, their future secure. Walt pursued his engineering degree uninterrupted by the draft, and Gracie continued her hospital training.

Gracie's three years at the Kansas State Agricultural College served to advance her in the University of Colorado's five-year combined course. She moved ahead rapidly in her training, and during her second year became night supervisor in charge of the hospital's first and second floors.

In these hours from eleven to seven she directed bedside nursing and chart entries, adminstered medications, checked surgical patients and changed dressings, kept an eye on critical conditions, reported to the physicians on duty, and compiled diet menus.

Seated now at a desk at the nurses' station on the first floor, Gracie looked at her watch. It was a quarter to three. She rose and picked up her tray of medicines. Walking noiselessly to the lower end of the hall, she began climbing the stairway to the second floor. A tall window at the center landing served to frame a pattern of stars that blazed in the night sky. Gracie stopped to gaze at the stars, captivated by their low-hung radiance, feeling she could almost reach out and touch them.

"Grace."

She felt a touch on her shoulder.

"Grace, you are working with effects. The cause is in the mind."

She turned. There was no one. The voice had spoken to her from within. Yet it had sounded about her, its tones shedding a quality of light, as if the stars themselves had addressed her.

She turned back to the window and looked again at the silent stars. Yes. This is what she had always felt, deep within herself, to be true; this is what she had somehow always known. The mind was the all-important factor, the precipitating cause, the source of physical manifestation.

Making her way up the remaining flight of stairs, Gracie was aware that a change had taken place within her. The desire to continue her career in medicine, in the nursing arts, had left her—had been suddenly lifted from her.

The experience remained in her mind for a long time. But eventually her duties—from delivering babies to assisting in emergency surgery—so claimed her that she rarely thought about it at all.

The weeks flew by. Almost before Gracie realized it, she was in her final semester, with only two months remaining until she would graduate from the University of Colorado's School of Nursing.

Then one evening in March, she received an emergency call from Fairy in Denver. It left her with no alternative but to go to her sister immediately. Their mother was in California with their father, who had persuaded Grace that, since the girls were now on their own, she should return with him to the west coast. William and Grace were not due back until June.

On the telephone now, Fairy, pregnant with her first child, was close to hysteria.

"Gracie—Gracie, you must come right away. Fred—is very ill. I'm so afraid, Gracie. The fever is going higher, and his breathing is terrible. Today he didn't know me—he didn't know I was there in the room with him. I don't know what to do. Gracie, you've got to help me! Please come right away. Please!"

Her voice broke and she began to cry.

"Fairy, you mustn't let yourself go to pieces like this. You mustn't cry so. It isn't good for you—for the baby. Fred needs your strength now. He needs you to be strong for him.

"I'll go to my supervisor right away. As soon as I can arrange to leave, I'll call you to tell you when I will be there."

Early the next morning Gracie went to the Director of Nurses' Office requesting an emergency consultation.

"You must go to them at once, of course," Miss Anderson told Gracie in her office. "But what a shame to have to interrupt your training at this point, Miss Lightfoot. You're just two months away from your Bachelor of Science degree and your R.N. license. However, come back as soon as possible to complete your training. We'll see to it that you pick up right where you left off. Go to your family now, my dear. And good luck to all of you."

For Fred Strout, the road to recovery was long. Little by

little, however, his strength returned under his sister-in-law's watchful care, and Gracie was able then to move to her parents' apartment on Monroe Street.

Regardless of the circumstances that brought her, having Gracie in Denver was a stroke of luck in Walter Pennock's opinion. His evenings with Gracie became more frequent as Fred's condition improved. The pair had dinner together, went to the theatre, to concerts, and walked the paths of picturesque Cheesman Park. When Fred and Fairy invited Walt and Gracie to dinner to celebrate Fred's recovery, it was the first of many good times the compatible foursome would share.

CHAPTER VII

DESTINY

At the end of his third year as crown and bridge instructor at the Harvard Dental School, Dr. Charles Patch resigned his position and went west to establish private practice in Denver.

The move had been a wise one. Dr. Patch enjoyed a sense of well-being in the rarefied Rocky Mountain region that he had never before experienced. Opening an office in downtown Denver, he went on to build a successful practice that attracted more patients each year.

"I must say Ben Cook knows his gems," Dr. Patch remarked now to his attractive young dental assistant, admiring the diamond ring that sparkled on the third finger of her left hand.

"So you would leave me to marry Ben Cook, eh? Well, *Mrs. Cook* is certainly an appropriate name for a wife. But what am I supposed to do without you? You're leaving me stranded, you know."

"*Stranded?* Dr. Patch! I gave you *two months' notice!* You haven't arranged for my replacement?"

"No, I haven't."

Ilma Love looked incredulously at the tall, distinguished-looking dentist for whom she'd worked two years.

"But—*why not?*"

"Oh, I guess I was holding out hoping you'd have a change of heart!"

They laughed, and Ilma said, "I'll miss being here, Dr. Patch. Working with you has been a pleasure and a privilege."

Her words were a tribute to the rapport between them. Ilma studied the face of the well-known Denver dentist with her direct brown eyes. Then she said,

"Dr. Patch—tell me something. Why have you never married?"

"Ah, the inevitable question! Well, the girl I'm looking for hasn't come along yet."

"What kind of girl would you like?"

"*What kind of girl would I like.*" Dr. Patch leaned back in his chair and looked up at the ceiling. "Well, let's see if I can tell you."

It had been more than nine years since he'd seen her. He wondered now if he could describe her.

"A nature girl. A girl who loves the outdoors. A girl who loves life and laughs a lot. Pretty, of course—with the sparkle of a mountain stream."

"Dr. Patch, that was beautiful! You know—you should meet *Gracie Lightfoot!*"

"Who?"

"Gracie Lightfoot—a high school friend of mine. She went away to college—Kansas, I believe—and after that I lost track of her."

"Hm. Well, that takes care of that. And now, Miss Love, back to work! Oh, yes. I'll prepare an ad for an assistant this morning and before you leave today please call it in to the *Post*. Have them run it for three days."

In her sister's home on High Street later that week, Gracie Lightfoot was combing the want ads of Denver's leading newspaper in search of a job.

"Gracie, this is my fault," Fairy said to her younger sister. "If I hadn't asked you to come home when Fred was ill, it wouldn't have happened. The trouble is that you've been away from your studies so long you don't want to settle down to them again."

"No, Fairy. My not going back to finish in nursing has nothing to do with coming home to help when Fred was ill. I won't have you thinking so. I could go back and pick up where I left off, easily. *But I don't want to. I've no desire to.*"

"But you were *crazy* about it! Is it that you want to stay in Denver because Walt's here?"

"That's not it either. I'm just no longer interested. I've no desire to go any further in nursing — in medicine."

"But *why?* What are Mama and Papa going to say? They're going to insist that you get your degree! Gracie, you're not being sensible. *You've only two months more!*"

"Fairy, I'm going to tell you something. Quite a while before Fred got sick, I had an — experience while on duty one night. After that I lost interest completely. I was able to see that I ended up in medicine because of a fascination with healing processes. You know — you cut a finger and it heals up. You break a bone and it knits together, good as new. You get sick, and there's a doctor with medicine or surgery to make you well. The power, the mystery behind it fascinated me. That's no longer the case."

Resistance gathered in Fairy's eyes, but before she could speak Gracie said firmly,

"I got as much out of nursing as I needed, and I've gone as far in medicine as I intend to go. I feel there's something else I'm to do now. And by golly I'd better get some kind of work soon, because when Mama and Papa find out, I'll be having to fend for myself! Now let me read the paper, Fairy. I want to see if there are any jobs in the want ads."

The next morning, Gracie walked along Sixteenth Street in her pale green linen suit, slowing her pace now and then to check building numbers. She was answering her first ad.

She came to the address written on the paper she held in her hand and turned into the walkway. The name on the shingle read: *Charles Warren Patch, D.D.S.* Gracie hesitated on the steps for a moment, then pressed the bell firmly.

The door opened and a man in a physician's coat stood there.

"Good morning," Charles Patch said, stunned as he looked into the face of the girl he had seen on the New Hampshire horizon at sunset nine years ago.

"Good morning. You advertised for a dental assistant?" Gracie managed to say, her mind repeating over and over: *"He's the one! He's the one!"*

"Yes. Please come in."

Gracie entered and Dr. Patch closed the door behind her.

"I'm Dr. Charles Patch," he said, smiling as he turned to her.

"How do you do, Dr. Patch. I'm Gracie Lightfoot."

"IIow do you do, Miss Lightfoot. Won't you sit down," he said, leading her to a chair near his desk.

He was a tall, slender man, tanned and strikingly handsome in his white coat. Reaching into a drawer, he brought out a sheet of paper.

"I'm with a patient now, Miss Lightfoot," he said. "But I have a form for you to fill out, if you will, please. You may sit here to write. And now if you will excuse me, I'll come back to you shortly," Charles Patch told her.

Gracie watched him as he left, then stared at the door he had closed behind him.

Alone in the hallway, Charles Patch stood as if in a dream. He shook off the feeling then and went to his waiting patient.

"He's the one. He's the one!" The words echoed again and again in Gracie's mind. She had seen this man before, and she knew exactly where and when. She had been in Miss Clark's eighth grade class in Manhattan, Kansas, when she

first saw him. She remembered being by the open window, looking out on the flat stretch of the horizon when he had suddenly appeared, seemingly out of the blue. He had smiled, humor crinkling the corners of his blue eyes, his straight, silver-gray hair glinting in the sunlight.

Gracie looked at the paper before her and reached for the pen. Concentrating on the words, she made the appropriate entries. Ending with her signature, she returned the pen to the inkstand.

The door opened and Dr. Patch came in. He took the paper Gracie held out to him and sat down, studying the form interestedly.

Her qualifications were very satisfactory, he remarked, and commended her on her background and training. He explained the duties, hours, and salary involved in the position — hers if she wished it — adding that she would be trained in dental techniques and procedures. He was presently without an assistant, Dr. Patch stated. If the job interested her, she could begin Monday of the following week.

She would accept the position, Gracie told Dr. Patch as the interview came to a close.

"Fine, Miss Lightfoot. Please come in Monday morning at a quarter to eight."

He walked with her to the door and briefly shook the hand Gracie held out to him. After she had gone, Charles Patch leaned against the door with closed eyes.

"Thank You." His lips formed the words. "She's lovely. Thank You."

Gracie walked quickly along Monroe Street toward her parents' apartment, happy about her new job. She was thrilled to have met Dr. Patch. She had been little more than a child nine years ago, when she'd had that vision of the man she would marry! With time she had forgotten about it. Today, answering an ad he had placed in the paper, she had walked into his office, qualified by background to become his assistant!

Dr. Charles Warren Patch. He was the one!

She walked up the steps, put the key in the lock, then froze.

Walt. Walt. Oh, Walt.

She let herself in, then went to her room and lay across her bed until night fell and the room was bathed in darkness.

As the weeks went by Gracie's pleasure in her new job was marred by severe migraine headaches. The headaches began after work each day and lasted into the night. Leaving her listless and without appetite, they intensified to the extent that she was unable to go out evenings. Three weeks passed and still Gracie had not seen Walt. Concerned about her, Walt telephoned her regularly and urged her to see a doctor.

Her parents worried. Gracie's headaches, they felt, were caused by the strain her new job placed upon her. They advised her to give it up. Noting their daughter's paleness at breakfast, they begged her one morning to take the day off. But Gracie insisted she could not.

At the office late that afternoon, Gracie cleared the counters, and as she stood at the cabinet replacing instruments, she thought about her parents' conversation that morning. Dr. Patch entered the inner office where Gracie was working and asked,

"Miss Lightfoot, will you have dinner with me tomorrow evening?"

Gracie hesitated, then turned to look at him.

"Yes," she said.

"Thank you. I seem to have been hanging in the balance there for a moment," he grinned.

Gracie laughed.

"That's a lot better," Charles Patch smiled, crossing the room to select from a shelf of impressions that lined a section of the wall.

The next evening William and Grace Lightfoot met Dr. Charles Patch, pleased that their daughter was going out for a few hours and relieved to see her looking better. Saturday evening Charles Patch called for Gracie again. Her evening engagements with the much older doctor became frequent. William and Grace appreciated Dr. Patch's professional interest in their young daughter, who was becoming well and happy again.

It was summer now. William Lightfoot continued to enjoy an extended vacation with his family before moving on to his new post in the east. In a few weeks, he and Grace would leave Denver for Washington, D.C., where he would staff a new office in the Department of the Interior.

Gracie came home one evening in late June to find the apartment dark and her parents out. Hearing voices through the open window, she went out to the side lawn where her mother and father sat talking. Gracie joined them, and after the three of them had talked for a time, she told her parents that she had become engaged that evening to Charles Patch.

The ring on her daughter's finger visible to her in the moonlight, Grace Lightfoot burst into tears. She begged Gracie to return the ring, to break off her relationship with the much older man.

William Lightfoot sat in silence, then rose abruptly and went indoors.

The next morning he confronted Gracie, his voice stern and disapproving.

"I forbid you to go through with this. The man is twenty-three years older than you — old enough to be your father. *Think, Gracie.* When you reach the prime of life, he will be an *old man* — or even *gone* — leaving you and your children alone. What's to become of you then? *I forbid it, Gracie. Understand that.*"

His reaction and her mother's hurt Gracie deeply. Her hurt

deepened as others denounced her engagement—Fairy, Fred, her friends. Gracie came home from work one evening to find Mabel Nickols waiting for her, her manner cold and condemning.

"Gracie—*Gracie, I can't believe this!* What in the world's come over you? *What about Walt? What about Walt, Gracie?* You couldn't hurt him like this! *You were in love!* What's this going to do to *Walt*?" Then she turned and left.

Walt telephoned Gracie. He had learned of her engagement, he told her. He wanted to see her. He would be there right away.

Stricken with intense migraine, Gracie met Walt at the door. They walked to the living room. She pulled the sliding doors closed behind her and leaned weakly against them.

"Gracie, I—*look at me, Gracie.*"

She raised her eyes.

"I *can't* let you marry somebody else. I *can't. What about us*, Gracie? *What about us? You're making a mistake!* This— doctor is *twice as old as you are*. Why are you doing this? *Why?*"

"It—just—happened this way, Walt. This—is something I must do. It—is right. It is—right for me. I do love you, Walt, but—but I'm going to learn a great deal from this man, Walt. Walt, please. Please understand."

"I'm to understand that you want to marry this man because you're going to learn a great deal from him? *Oh, my God*, Gracie! That doesn't make *sense*!"

Tears gathered in Gracie's eyes and she dropped her gaze.

"I'm hurting you," he said. "I don't want to do that, Gracie."

He moved past her and through the doors. They closed behind him and he was gone.

CHAPTER VIII

DR. NONA L. BROOKS, MINISTER

The little brick building sat far back on the lot at Seventeenth and Clarkson Streets. It held a peculiar fascination for Gracie. Each time she passed it she felt a pull toward it. She wondered how she came to notice it in the first place, for it was no different from other brick buildings that lined the streets everywhere. Yet each time she went by on the streetcar she would gaze at it curiously. Riding by with her fiancé one day, she turned to him and said,

"Charles — see that little brick building there? Do you know anything about it? I feel a strange pull toward that place. Do you know what it is?"

"Yes. Would you like to go there?"

"I would! What is it?"

"That's the First Divine Science Church and College of Denver."

"What does that mean?"

"Just what it says. It's a church, and a college. It's a teaching church. It offers spiritual education. People can go there to study."

"What does it teach?"

"Divine Science. The principle and practice of Divine Science. The Principle of Truth."

"How do you know about that place, Charles?"

"Well, the minister there is a very dear friend of mine. At one time I was superintendent of her Sunday School."

63

"*Her* Sunday School? The minister is a *woman*?"

Charles smiled. "Yes. Quite a woman! And quite a minister! We'll go there Sunday and you can meet her—Dr. Nona L. Brooks."

Gracie entered the red brick building Sunday morning intrigued. In appearance the church was unlike any she had ever seen. Rows of wooden chairs lined both sides of the narrow space that served as a center aisle. A stove, piano, lectern, and speaker's chair were the only other objects in the room. Light, softly diffused, filled the little meeting place.

Later as they were riding home Gracie said to Charles,

"There's something peculiar about this! Last night while we were talking, you told me practically everything Dr. Brooks said in her sermon this morning! Now how could you have known what she would say?"

"It's because I was one of her students for a long time, Grace. I studied with Dr. Brooks for several years. When I read the title of her sermon in the paper, I could judge what material would be included and the ideas she would bring out. Well, what did you think of Dr. Brooks, Grace?"

"She's a beautiful person. There's something about her, Charles. What is it? It almost seemed as if she were speaking a different language. I didn't understand half of what she said."

Charles smiled. "You need another go at it or so. I'll take you again next week."

"It seemed strange to hear a minister talk like that. So *certain*, so *serene*. She says things that are new and different—that sound too good to be true! Yet—somehow it all struck me as right. And the people—they seem so *loving*. And they all seemed to have a kind of—*light*. I'd like to go again, Charles."

"All right, Grace. It's a date."

Charles always called her *Grace*. She liked that. And eleven days later on July 19, Grace Lightfoot became Mrs. Charles Patch.

On a bright afternoon three weeks after her marriage, Grace answered a knock at the door to find her high school principal standing there.

"Mr. Pearson! What a lovely surprise. Please come in," she said.

"Thank you, Mrs. Patch." Mr. Pearson greeted her with a smile she remembered well. "I came to bring you my best wishes. I learned from Ilma Love Cook that you became a bride recently."

"How nice of you, Mr. Pearson! Thank you." Grace extended her hand to the kindly administrator. "Please come into the living room and we'll have a cup of tea," she said, leading him to the sofa and taking the chair to his right. "Are you vacationing in Denver, Mr. Pearson?"

"No, we're living here now. I resigned from the Cripple Creek school system two years ago and joined the staff at East Denver High. I teach History and Government there."

"It's almost impossible to think of you in a school other than Cripple Creek High, Mr. Pearson!"

"I was there a good many years. I remember when your sister joined our faculty there in Cripple. As you know, Cripple Creek has all but come to a halt. Mrs. Pearson and I and our children began to feel pretty isolated there as time went by. So we decided to buy a home in Denver. We're happy here."

"I'm glad, Mr. Pearson. A lot of Cripple Creek people are living in Denver now, I understand.

"Mr. Pearson, please excuse me for a few minutes while I put on some tea for us," Grace said, rising to go to the kitchen.

She returned soon to serve her guest.

"So you've seen Ilma Love Cook here in Denver, Mr. Pearson," she remarked interestedly.

"Yes. Ilma told me you were living here, and that your husband is the dentist she worked for before her marriage."

"Ilma and I were close friends in high school. I had no idea, though, that she worked here in Denver, nor that it was she I was replacing when I went to work for Dr. Patch. When Charles told me his former assistant's name, I was so surprised!"

"I have a young friend studying dentistry here in Denver, Gracie, who will graduate in June. He was telling me the other evening that there's a dentist in this city who is known as the best crown and bridge man west of the Mississippi — Dr. Charles Patch. I wanted to mention that to you."

"Thank you, Mr. Pearson. Charles is a fine dentist. He taught for some time in the Harvard Dental School — his alma mater — before coming west."

Grace rose to pour more tea for her guest.

"Are your parents here in Denver, Gracie?"

"Not now. They were for a time. Then my father was taken off the field — he was a cadastral engineer with the U.S. Geological Survey — and given an office in the Department of the Interior. So he and mother are in Washington, D.C. now."

"Washington is a beautiful city. I've been there, and I'd like to go back again sometime."

"I've never been to Washington, Mr. Pearson. I've never been east of the Mississippi River. They like it. Mother writes us that, almost every time she goes out, she sees a famous person! She's been there little more than a month, and already she's glimpsed President Wilson in person! Also Amelia Earhart, on the steps of the National Geographic Building!"

"Good for her!"

"Fairy lives here, Mr. Pearson. They have a home on High Street."

"I haven't seen Fairy for three years. How is she?"

"Well, Fairy is a new mother. She gave birth to twin babies two weeks ago—a boy and a girl."

"Wonderful! They are all coming along well?"

"I wish I could say so, Mr. Pearson. There were some complications. Fairy isn't getting along as well as she should. We're—very concerned about her. Dr. Dunwoody asked us to call Mama and Papa. They're coming in day after tomorrow."

"Oh, I'm sorry. I hope all will be well. I mustn't stay any longer, Gracie," Mr. Pearson said. "Please remember me to your husband and family. Please give them my best."

"I will. Thank you. It meant so much to have you here this afternoon, Mr. Pearson. You are my first guest since my marriage. It was a very special pleasure, indeed. Please come back again."

When William and Grace Lightfoot arrived two days later they found their new grandchildren lying in their cradles screaming in red-faced protest and flailing the air with tiny fists as Dr. Dunwoody came down the hall from their mother's room to call the family to her bedside. The infants' cries intensified fifteen minutes later as their father made his way out of the room and down the stairs to his study.

William Lightfoot gathered his broken-hearted wife to him and took her from the room. Dr. Dunwoody held Gracie against his shoulder, then asked her to help the nurse quiet the babies. He closed the door after her to stand alone with his thoughts.

Frances Lee Lightfoot Strout, young, beautiful, with everything to live for, had died at thirty-one.

Fred Strout, twice widowered in twelve years, stayed alone in his study. At intervals his father-in-law entered to sit with him.

The twin babies had turned colicky and refused to take their milk. They sensed the bereaved atmosphere in the home, Dr. Dunwoody explained. He suggested they be taken elsewhere before they began losing the ground gained in their two weeks of life. His advice fell on deaf ears.

When Ernest and Alice Smith arrived from Oregon for the funeral of their cousin, Alice entered the nursery and lost her heart to the beautiful babies. That afternoon she relieved the nurse, noting her need for rest. By evening, the infants stopped their crying and sucked hungrily at their milk.

It was to Alice Smith and her lawyer-husband Ernest that Fred Strout made one of his few attempts at words after his wife's funeral. The day before their departure, Alice and Ernest entered Fred's study to find him alone by the window.

"Fred, forgive us for intruding," Ernest began.

Fred did not turn to acknowledge their presence.

"Fred, please try to understand what we want to say. Alice and I have no children. According to our doctor we never will have children of our own. It's a great disappointment to us.

"If you would consider it, Fred, we would like to take the babies home to Oregon with us. It's a difficult thing to ask, a difficult thing to ask of you. They would receive the finest care—every possible advantage. We—would like you to think about it."

Fred made no response. Ernest and Alice went out, leaving him alone in the darkening study.

"Yes," Fred told them as they were ready to leave for Oregon the following day. "Yes—you may take the babies."

CHAPTER IX

A STUDENT OF TRUTH

It was autumn now. Charles and Grace Patch sat in their living room watching the twilight surrender to the night. Charles put another log on the fire, standing at the hearth for a time as the glowing embers sputtered and flared beneath the fresh-laid wood.

He came back to the sofa and Grace pulled the cord of the bridge lamp, lighting the corner where he would read. Charles reached for *The American Dental Association Journal* which had come that day and became absorbed in its contents.

He broke off from his reading when he realized Grace was crying.

"Grace? What is it?"

But he knew. It was a month today since Fairy's death. Grace's mother had stayed on at the Strout home after William had returned to Washington, but would be leaving tomorrow for the east. He and Grace would take her to the train station in the morning.

"I hate to see Mama go away feeling like this, Charles. She's so *embittered*. It's not healthy. And it's not *like* Mama. She's very much against God now. She's blaming God. She keeps saying that God shouldn't have taken Fairy away—that this was the time she was needed most by her babies and her husband. I think she has—rejected God. She should be looking to God for comfort—for support. But she's not doing that."

69

"Well, she's deeply grieved, of course. But she's wasting her energy, blaming God. God *per se* had nothing to do with it. Now, if your mother is rejecting the *concept* of a God who sends death and sickness and tragedy, that's something *else*. That's healthy. I go along with that one hundred per cent. To a thinking person, looking for comfort from a God who sent the trouble in the first place *would* be difficult — paradoxical. No intelligent person could warm up to a God like that. No intelligent person truly could love or worship or even respect a God like that. If your mother is at *that* point in realization, she's on the right track. She's moving in the right direction. She'll be all right."

The next morning Charles and Grace saw her mother aboard the train for Washington, then waited in Union Station until the train had passed from sight. Parting had been difficult for both women.

"A different environment will be the best thing for her," Charles reassured Grace as they rode to the office. "A change is what you need, too, Grace. We're going to the mountains tomorrow for a weekend of camping and fishing. Dr. Patch's orders."

During their courtship, Charles and Grace had often spent a Saturday or Sunday in the neighboring mountains. Closing the office at noon on Saturday, they would load their gear into Charles' old Ford and ride into the Rockies, returning at dark. Sundays they enjoyed an earlier start and arrived in the mountains soon after sunrise.

After Grace's first visit to the little church at Seventeenth and Clarkson they postponed their Sunday jaunts until noon so that Grace could hear Dr. Brooks' sermons.

"Two days in the mountains? *Oh, yes, Charles!* Except for one thing — I don't want to miss hearing Dr. Brooks Sunday morning."

"You've really done an about face, Grace. When I met you, you didn't *like* to go to church! Tell you what. We'll take a book along and have an hour of Divine Science ourselves Sunday morning, right up there in the mountains."

Charles could appreciate the interest Divine Science held for his young wife. He had experienced the same reaction when he first became aware of its enlightening principle.

He smiled now as he recalled what had happened on their way to church the previous Sunday. They'd not gone a block when his temperamental Ford began to sputter and choke, finally slowing to a stop. After lifting the hood to search out the trouble, he'd looked at Grace and said,

"I have a carburetor problem. This is going to take some time. We won't make it to church this morning, Grace."

"Oh, I'm sorry, Charles. Is there anything I can do?"

"Not a thing. I'll take care of it."

"Then—do you mind if I walk to church? I can make it if I hurry."

"Ah, but ladies don't go to church without their husbands," he'd teased her.

"Well, this one does. I'll walk home, too, Charles. I'd like to. It's a beautiful morning."

She went on, the first time since their marriage that she'd gone anywhere without him.

"I'm home!" Grace thought as she entered the little church on Clarkson Street. She'd experienced the same reaction the first time she had attended—the feeling that she had come *home*. Alone now, she chose a seat in the last row where she could sit unnoticed. It took all of her powers of concentration to understand Dr. Brooks' statements. Their contents challenged every concept and viewpoint she'd been taught in the past. Dr. Brooks' interpretation of the Principle of Omnipresence intrigued her.

That night, Grace recounted the substance of Dr. Brooks' sermon to Charles. Then she plied him with questions. Would he please explain the *Law*? Dr. Brooks was always talking about the *Law*. And Consciousness. Omnipresence. Principle.

Truth. Cause and effect. Infinite Mind. One Mind. Oneness. Substance. Spirit. The Absolute.

"All right," he laughed. "One at a time. I'll do my best, Grace. But you need a teacher. It's time you began to study. We'll see about getting you a teacher the next time we go to church."

The Sunday following their weekend in the mountains Charles and Grace arrived in church early. During the prelude Charles murmured, "Look around and choose someone you'd like to study with — any one of the older ones. Most of them are teachers."

Grace studied the faces within her range of vision. *"How,"* she thought, *"am I to know which of them is the teacher for me?"*

By eleven o'clock the room was filled with people and Dr. Brooks rose to stand at the lectern. Grace abandoned her search and gave full attention to the service. She followed the sermon closely, making mental notes of points she would ask Charles to clarify later.

The hour passed quickly. Soon they were singing the closing hymn and standing for Dr. Brooks' benediction.

Charles and Grace mingled with the congregation, greeting friends and newcomers. Within minutes they were surrounded by those wanting a word with Charles. Others lingered to exchange a handshake.

"Charles certainly has a way with people," Grace thought, watching her husband talking amiably with those around him. It was the same wherever they went. At any gathering Charles was always the life of the party. She was proud of him and admired him tremendously. And she was perfectly content to sit in the background observing his charm as he invariably carried the conversation with one amusing story after another.

Turning, Grace found herself beside a serene, pleasant-faced woman who greeted her with,

"Good morning, my dear. I'm Jessie Bromfield. It's good to see you here."

"Thank you, Mrs. Bromfield. I'm Grace Patch."

"*Oh, you're Charles' wife, then!* I've known Charles for a long time. He is *wonderful*."

"Mrs. Bromfield, would it be possible for me to study with you?"

There was a rapport, a bond between them that they both recognized. The woman hesitated, then she said, "I'm not a teacher, my dear."

"But could you teach me? I'm very much interested in this Science and want to learn as much as I possibly can about it."

Charles came over then.

"I see you two have already met," he said. "Mrs. Bromfield, let's find a teacher for Grace. She'd like to study, but can't enroll in a regular class. She's too full of questions. She'd hold the group back. Grace will have to study privately."

"We were just talking about that, Charles," Mrs. Bromfield told him. "I'll ask Dr. Brooks about it. Perhaps I can give her private instruction. We'll see. We will need Dr. Brooks' approval, of course."

Later as they walked along Clarkson Street toward their car, Charles said, "Mrs. Bromfield is a minister, Grace. She taught for a long time before she was ordained. You couldn't have made a better choice!"

"She mentioned that Dr. Brooks would have to approve the arrangement."

"Yes, and I'm sure she will."

Wednesday evening they received a call from Mrs. Bromfield. Dr. Brooks had approved private lessons in Divine Science Principle for Grace.

Notebook and pencil in hand, Grace went to Mrs. Bromfield's home each Tuesday and Thursday afternoon. In the serenity of Mrs. Bromfield's study they read and discussed the subject matter of the lessons she had prepared for Grace.

Grace's questions concerning Divine Science Principle seemed endless; still, Mrs. Bromfield answered patiently and encouraged her young student to ask to her heart's content.

In the evenings Grace reviewed the lessons with Charles, listening intently as he clarified concepts that seemed to her implausible or unduly abstract. Often they talked until two or three o'clock in the morning. Sometimes Grace would argue a point, not to be argumentative but because she wanted to *know*, to understand the underlying concept completely. The Principle of Divine Science, Omnipresence, had become comprehensible to her as the Great-Three-in-One— Religion, Science, and Philosophy. Comprehending, she felt she was home—home at last after a long, inquiring journey. Now, however, there was still the need to question it, analyze it, challenge it. She had to be sure that the Principle held water, so to speak. She had to test its practicality, find out if it really worked.

"Grace, there's an advantage to private study, sure—but I don't want you to miss the fun of group exchange," Charles said after a lively discussion one evening. "There's a great deal of stimulation and enjoyment in getting together with others interested in this teaching. Let's invite another couple or two to come in Friday nights for home study. We'll choose a good book to read and discuss—maybe Thomas Troward's *Edinburgh Lectures*."

Margie and Jack Heberling and Janet and Ken Miller came the next Friday, bringing such enthusiasm to the session that the two hours seemed to fly. Judge Troward's book was new to all of them. They made their way through it slowly, reading aloud in turn and stopping frequently to discuss the longer, more involved sentences.

As the weeks went by Grace tossed most of her long-held concepts onto the scrap heap. Heaven and hell were no longer places to which one was assigned in the sweet by and by, but

states of consciousness experienced in the here and now —
characterized by peace, harmony, happiness, freedom, and
well-being on the one hand; and fear, pain, trouble, anger,
hatred, sorrow, and limitation on the other. The Judgmen-
tal Figurehead sitting on a throne somewhere in the remote
skies that she had been taught to look up to as God —
bestowing His blessings on some and withholding them from
others — was replaced by Omnipresence, the All-Present One;
Omniscience, the All-Knowing One; Omnipotence, the All-
Powerful One; Divine Love; Truth; Principle; The Absolute;
Universal Being; The One Power; God, synonymous with
Good. Luck, fate, chance, and superstition crumbled under
the comprehensive Law of Cause and Effect, the Law of At-
traction: Like Begets Like.

It came as a flash, seemingly, that moment when she realized Who and What God is. In that moment she felt deep inner peace; well-being; freedom; renewal; love; and gratitude.
She knew then who she was, who others were — not mere pup-
pets manipulated by forces beyond their control, nor autom-
atons functioning at the whim and will of some inscrutable
power, but offspring of the Most High; Children of God, Omnipresent Good; endowed with the divine qualities of Love,
Wisdom, Knowledge, Understanding, Power, Life, and Joy;
equipped by grace to learn and co-operate with the laws of
the Universe for their individual unfoldment, fulfillment, and
happiness.

Her common sense confirmed this. It was reasonable, it was
intelligent. The awareness of this new-found joy brought with
it new responsibility. It called for a complete reassessment and
realignment of thought patterns, opinions, outlooks, habits,
and attitudes. It called for discipline.

Three days before their first wedding anniversary, Charles
and Grace closed the office to vacation for two weeks in the
mountains. They camped and hiked in the breathtaking set-

tings of the Rockies, fishing for meal fare and sleeping under the stars at night. Moving onward and upward each day, they followed pine-flanked trails to grassy clearings bordered by spruce groves and slender aspens. It was midsummer, and wildflowers bloomed in colorful profusion. The pair set up camp wherever the scenery held them, then moved on.

Conversation was punctuated by awe at the beauty lying all about them, its mystique changing with each hour. Mostly they moved along in silence, tuned to the surrounding stillness broken only by the songs of birds, the call of a coyote, owl, or mountain lion, the scurrying of small creatures.

Spent from the day, the pair slept early, rising just before dawn to bathe in the night-warmed waters of a lake or stream. With the rising of the sun Charles stalked small game for breakfast or fished while Grace gathered wood and set the fire. They ate heartily of bluebass, rainbow trout, quail, pheasant, or rabbit. Watercress, wheat wafers, wild grapes or berries, and spring water rounded out their meal.

"Charles, I wish this didn't have to end," Grace said when it was time to go back to Denver. "We've had a wonderful time! And it's done you so much good. You look marvelous!"

He did. His blue eyes sparkled in his tanned face, its ruddy tones a stunning contrast to his silver-gray hair. From the hour they'd left Denver two weeks ago, Grace had seen tension literally fall away from her husband as they drove toward the mountains. Charles had been born to the outdoors. She understood the effect the four walls of the office had on this high-spirited, freedom-loving man. After a time they "closed in on him," leaving him tense, nervous, restless for the outdoors.

"This is a lifestyle like no other," Charles responded. "Five years ago I closed the office and came up to these mountains to live for two years. I took work wherever I found it—as a forest ranger, game warden, crop-harvester. I had the time of my life! I went back and reopened the office, satisfied for a while. I can stand at that chair only a certain length of time, Grace. Then I have to get away."

"But what about your practice? What did your patients do while you were away?"

"They saw another dentist until I got back."

"They didn't mind that?"

"They're my friends as well as my patients. No, they didn't mind."

Two days later they were in Denver, with office hours as usual.

When Dr. Nona Brooks learned that Charles and Grace had returned, she dropped by the office one afternoon to see them.

"Dr. Brooks! What a lovely surprise!" Grace greeted her.

"I was passing by and thought I'd check on my children. It's good to have you home again. I'll see you both Sunday morning, I trust, and in class Thursday evening."

"Oh, yes. Stay awhile, Nona," Charles told her. "My next patient isn't due for half an hour. Why not come to the chair and have an examination?"

"Now, Charles. I don't need an examination. *I* know that and *you* should know that. I see myself as perfect. What are you seeing?"

"I'll tell you after I've examined your teeth," Charles grinned. "Come on. Be a sport."

She had three cavities.

"*Three cavities!*" Nona Brooks exclaimed incredulously. "*Hm!* Well, *that's what I get for hanging around people like you!*" Her eyes twinkled and her laughter rang out.

"Well, Nona, why don't we demonstrate?" Charles suggested. "Why don't we let the Law work? Why not let the Law flow into expression, have the right of way in this—since perfection is our dream, our desire, and our right? I'll clean out the cavities, but I won't fill them. We'll treat for the filling of the cavities to be a natural thing. We'll work together on it."

"All right. Go ahead. Clean out the cavities and leave it at that. All things are possible, son, to those who love God, Omnipresent Good, including the restoration of the enamel of the teeth."

Walking with their minister to the door, Grace said,

"Dr. Brooks, we're looking forward to your message Sunday. We'll see you then."

"Oh! We're having a guest speaker next Sunday — Dr. Harry Gaze. Dr. Gaze is an outstanding English New Thought lecturer and author. You're in for a treat, children."

They found Harry Gaze fascinating. In his talk the itinerant teacher of Practical Metaphysics made reference to his long, close association with Judge Thomas Troward, the renowned English metaphysician and author whose book, *The Edinburgh Lectures*, was the text the Patches used in their home study sessions earlier that year.

Dr. Gaze's dynamic, mind-expanding ideas concerning life, health, and immortality had his listeners standing in line for a word with him and a clasp of his hand after the service had ended.

Thrilled at the capacity audience the lecture had drawn, Dr. Nona Brooks stood at the church entrance talking with Charles and Grace.

"Are you comfortable?" Charles asked Dr. Brooks in a low tone.

"Is there any reason why I shouldn't be comfortable?" she questioned, her eyes twinkling.

"No. No, there isn't."

"Very well, then. Keep true to your Basis, Charles. Remain true to the Principle of Omnipresence, my son. And according to your faith it shall be done unto you — *according to your steadfast faith in Omnipresent Good.*"

Dr. Gaze came to stand with them then.

"Shall we tell him? Let's tell him so that he can rejoice with us," Nona Brooks said, and in quiet tones she shared with her colleague the treatment of the cavities.

They had dinner together as Dr. Brooks' guests, then they saw Dr. Gaze to his hotel. He would leave on the evening train for Kansas City.

On a subsequent visit to Denver, Dr. Harry Gaze strode into Nona Brooks' office and commanded his friend, "All right now! Open, so I can see for myself!"

"Oh!" she laughed. "Why certainly! Come over here by the window."

The teeth had completely filled. The enamel was perfectly restored. Deeply moved, Harry Gaze exclaimed softly, "Praise the Lord, the Law of All Good!"

Before saying goodbye, Dr. Gaze asked permission to include the account of "the teeth filled by faith" in the lecture material for his next world tour. It was granted. Within fourteen months thousands at home and abroad were told the story of the teeth filled by faith.

The restoration of Nona Brooks' teeth baffled Grace.

"Charles, if I hadn't seen it with my own eyes I wouldn't believe it," she told her husband as they opened the office the next morning. "*Teeth filled naturally!* Impossible!"

"No, Grace. Not when one has the high consciousness Nona Brooks has—not when one has a realization of oneness with the Presence, as Nona Brooks has."

"But this is a *phenomenon! She's a walking miracle!*"

"In the eyes of most of us, yes. But to those in Divine Science, miracles—healings—are natural and right occurrences, the results of realized perfection. They're expected. That's not the first of Nona Brooks' miracles, Grace. I've heard her tell of others."

"You have? Tell me about them."

"I'll tell you on the way home this evening," he told Grace as the bell rang and his first patient entered.

Charles saw his last patient out at five-thirty that day, then he and Grace cleaned and closed the office.

As they walked home, Charles began, "Nona Brooks experienced her first healing when she was much younger. She had ulcers of the throat, and for a long time could eat only very soft, specially prepared foods. Although she'd had extensive medical treatment, the condition worsened. Finally her doctor told her that he had done all he could for her. Her weight had gone down to eighty-five pounds and she could barely swallow at all. She and her family had to face the fact that the end was near.

"Then a friend of theirs who had heard that Nona was terminally ill visited them one day. She was Mrs. Frank Bingham, and she had been healed of a long and serious illness in Chicago through the spiritual help of Mrs. Emma Curtis Hopkins.

"Grateful for the healing she had received, Mrs. Bingham was offering a class in her home based on the teachings and healing methods of Mrs. Hopkins. She asked the Brooks family to come. It would mean recovery for Nona, she insisted. The Brooks women were skeptical but by this time they were willing to try anything. They accepted her invitation.

"The basic principle Mrs. Bingham taught in her classes was Omnipresence. Omnipresence, the Presence of God, All Good, everywhere, all of the time, in everybody, in everything. She instructed her students to live with the word *Omnipresence*, the Omnipresence of God, God being synonymous with Good. She urged them to keep the concept of All Good Omnipresent uppermost in their minds, their thoughts, at all times. She gave them statements to dwell on: *God, All Good, is All. God, All Good, is Everywhere, therefore God, All Good, is here. God, Omnipresent Good, is Health. Omnipresent Good which is Omnipresent Health includes me in its health. Only God, All Good, is real, and God is Health. Only Health is real.*

"In Horatio Dresser terms Mrs. Bingham told her class that, '. . . there is a truth not generally known, the understanding of which tends to avoid sickness and leads to health and happiness. It is an eternal truth . . . the understanding of which can be supplied through teaching and practice . . . it is natural and right to be well, and the simple truth, understood and applied, destroys the error of disease.'

"That Truth, Mrs. Bingham brought her students to understand, is Omnipresence.

"Knowing her health was failing fast, Nona Brooks and her sister Alethea immediately began practicing the concept of Omnipresence according to Mrs. Bingham's instructions. The two of them affirmed it and held to it at all times in all situations and conditions.

"During the fourth class with Mrs. Bingham, Nona Brooks experienced a dramatic healing. Right there in Mrs. Bingham's living room, suddenly her whole being was flooded with light—an intense white light 'brighter than sunlight,' as she described it. At the time, she thought the others too were seeing that light. But later she learned that they hadn't—that only she had seen it. The moment she experienced that flood of light, she was completely healed of her terminal illness and restored to perfect health—instantly."

"Oh, Charles," Grace said, "I knew there was something special about Dr. Brooks the moment I saw her. She *radiates light*—and *love*, and *happiness*! Charles, this teaching fascinates me! I want to learn as much about it as I possibly can— as *fast* as I can!"

"Well, just keep taking the classwork and apply what you learn as well as you can. It takes practice, Grace—practice and discipline."

"I'm enjoying Dr. Brooks' class tremendously. Now that I know about her healing, it will be more meaningful than ever. But there's one thing that bothers me, Charles—one thing that I simply can't go along with. She says that sickness and disease are false beliefs—that they are *not real!*"

"You see, Grace, you're approaching it from the standpoint of the intellect, which is relative, rather than from the standpoint of Truth, or Omnipresence, which is Absolute."

"Charles, *nobody* can tell *me* that disease isn't *real! I've seen it!*"

"Refusing to believe in disease, Nona Brooks explains, does not mean that it has no existence in *appearance*," Charles said. "It means that there is no real or permanent *cause* for such an appearance. Jesus put it this way, *Judge not according to the appearance* (relative), *but judge righteous judgment* (Absolute). He knew the relative nothingness of disease; and He knew the Absolute Allness of Health. There are people in the world today, and Nona Brooks is one of them, who, through a high consciousness of God as Omnipresent Good—and a realization of oneness with Omnipresent Good —know the nothingness of disease. Health is *normal*, Grace. Disease is *abnormal*, and can be voided by a realization of the Grand Normal, Omnipresence."

Turning onto Monroe Street, they were two blocks from home now.

"Please go on, Charles," Grace said.

"The universe and everything in it is governed by Law. Strange as it may sound, our beliefs become laws unto ourselves. In the King James Version of the Bible, the book of Proverbs states it this way: *As a man thinketh in his heart, so is he.* Another translation of the Bible puts it this way: *I will be a God unto you according to your own hearts.* And Jesus said it this way: *According to your belief it shall be done unto you.*

"Divine Science presents God as Omnipresent Good; Infinite Substance, All Good, in which there is no absence of

Good. The truth that God does not recognize disease, evil or error is underscored by the Bible: *God is of purer eyes than to behold evil, and canst not look on iniquity.*"

"Then why do people become ill? Why was Nona Brooks ill? Why was I ill most my life until I began studying Truth?" Grace contended.

"Through ignorance we misinterpret things, Grace. We form false concepts of life, and consequently we live, express, and experience according to our misconceptions. Actually, most people's troubles stem from a belief in an anthropomorphic God—a kind of super-inflated version of themselves—an unfathomable Supreme Being capable at His discretion of sending both sickness and disease, health and healing. When there is this dual concept of the nature of God, there is a dual flow of expression in the life of the individual. Truth, Omnipresence, voids the concept of a dual-natured God. This right concept of God makes for a right relationship with God. It is this concept of God as Ominpresent Good—*and the realization of oneness with God*—that heals. When we can realize that *what God is, man is*, then we're on our way to demonstrating our heritage—our Divine Heritage—of Perfect Good."

CHAPTER X

A ROCKY MOUNTAIN IDYLL

Charles and Grace were expecting their first baby. Elated at the prospect of becoming a father, Charles said to his wife,

"Grace, let's not stay around this town listening to a lot of old wives' tales while waiting for our baby to be born. None of that for *us*! Let's go up to the mountains and have our baby there—away from all negatives—away from all do's and don'ts! We want Truth, Omnipresence, to be our baby's only prenatal influence."

"Charles! Wouldn't it be wonderful if we could do that?"

"We *can* do it, and we will."

"But how? What about your practice?"

"My patients can go to another dentist while we're away."

"I don't know, Charles. They might not like—"

"It'll work out all right! My patients are my patients. They'll still be my patients when we get back."

"Charles, I love the mountains so! What an experience that would be—having our baby up there in those gorgeous Rockies. It would be heaven on earth!"

"At Harvard, Grace, my two best friends were in Obstetrics-Gynecology. I was very interested, so with special permission they let me observe birth deliveries occasionally. I learned a great deal by watching what was happening and what was being done. With that, and with your background in nursing, there's no reason why we couldn't handle it."

"*I know we could!* We can get everything we need for the delivery at Lane Bryant right here before we leave. Between the two of us, we'll do fine. *The father will be the doctor and the mother will be the nurse!*"

One month later the pair began their journey. They went from Denver to Cripple Creek. Grace wanted to start there, where she was born, and where she had shared so many happy times with her high school friends. Their train came to a stop at Cripple's Midland Terminal and Grace and Charles stepped down to the platform. As they waited for their baggage Grace looked down Bennett Avenue, her eyes following the path she'd taken to Cripple Creek High, Welty and Faulkner's Grocery Store, Mt. Pisgah, and the homes of her friends.

They checked their bags and walked across the street to look down into the little valley below. There winding its way along was Cripple Creek, the little stream that gave the town its name. They moved along Bennett Avenue then, past the courthouse toward the frame house at 307 May Street where Grace was born.

Suddenly Grace stopped.

"Grace, what's the matter?" Charles asked.

"*It—it isn't there!* Our house is gone—*they've torn it down!*" Grace told him. Tears came as she gazed at the place where her home had been.

"That's too bad, Grace. It looks like they've graded over a large area there. They must be planning to build something big. Well, things don't stay the way they were forever," Charles said, putting an arm around her shoulder. "Come on. We'd better see about getting a place to stay while we're here. Then I want a tour of the World's Greatest Gold Camp!"

They rented a small cabin for ten dollars a month, planning to stay in Cripple Creek until they found two suitable burros and the equipment they would need for their journey by foot through the mountains.

Then, starting at Tenderfoot Hill, Grace treated her husband to a tour of the old mining town, where prospectors from every part of the country appeared in the early days, seeking their fortunes in gold; pick-and-shovel-bearing men from all walks of life — doctors, lawyers, businessmen, grocers, bricklayers, barbers.

From atop Tenderfoot Hill they looked down on the five-hundred-resident community of Cripple Creek. Beyond Cripple rose spruce-capped Mt. Pisgah, and at its base lay Pisgah Cemetery, the gold camp's burial ground since 1892. Turning, the pair could see the snow-laced crests of the Sangre de Cristo Range extending south into New Mexico.

They made their way downhill to the *Molly Kathleen*, famous for its two million-dollar yield in gold ore. South of the mine was Poverty Gulch, site of the original gold strike made by Bob Womack. Here Grace pointed to the spot where her parents had lived in a cabin during the gold rush until they could buy a house.

They wandered through the section called "Old Town," then along the buildings at Fourth and Bennett which had been assay offices long ago. One of these had been her brother-in-law's, Grace told Charles, pointing out the place which had been Fred's.

On the corner across the street was the building that was once the Cripple Creek Gold-Mining Exchange, and north of it stood Cripple Creek High School. They headed for the school then, moving along a paved incline edged by an iron handrail.

"As a schoolgirl I held to this rail on slippery days, pulling myself to the top," Grace reminisced, running a hand along its length.

They strolled around the school and back to Bennett Avenue, past the Central Fire Station and City Hall. Next door was The First National Bank of Cripple Creek. Here

Grace pointed to the second story, in Cripple's heydey the elegant apartment of mining king A. E. Carlton and his glamorous wife.

They went on, then paused at the *Gold Rush* building, home of Cripple Creek's newspaper. Cripple's original newspaper had been *The Crusher*, Grace explained, and its first issue had been printed in gold ink.

Grace directed Charles' attention across the street to Johnny Nolon's, the finest of the gold camp's saloons and gambling houses.

"You're quite a guide, Grace," Charles told her. "This is interesting."

They swung around the corner to Myers Avenue, once Cripple Creek's notorious red-light district. Before them stood *The Old Homestead*, the grandest and only remaining of the parlour houses that had flourished along Myers Avenue.

They walked back to Bennett Avenue, past the Imperial Hotel, and stood looking up at St. Peter's Church, built atop Cripple's highest hill. Then they were at the corner of Second and Bennett, the old trolley's turning point for neighboring Victor, where Grace and her friends saw vaudeville shows or spent an evening at the Victor Opera House.

Wandering down the Welty block, the pair dropped into Welty and Faulkner's Grocery and bought a few staples for their cupboard. They continued down Bennett to the Teller County Courthouse, built during Cripple's boom when Cripple Creek was made county seat. Next they peered into the Cripple Creek jail, called *Hotel Detain* by its residents.

"You do very well by your home town," Charles told Grace.

They wound up their sightseeing with a stroll through Pisgah Cemetery, resting place of early fortune hunters, and residents who had chosen to stay on after the gold camp's decline, making Cripple Creek their home. Wildflowers and berry vines bloomed among the gravesites and along the quaint iron fences, clinging to now elaborately ornate, now starkly simple tombstones robbed by time of identifying marks.

Then taking the pathway that lay to the left, Charles and Grace walked down the road to the little cabin that was their temporary home.

Within two weeks they found and purchased two burros, saddles, and the camping equipment needed for their journey. They were ready to depart.

A rooster crowed behind them as Charles and Grace led their pack burros beyond Cripple Creek, its outbursts growing fainter as they made their way farther and farther down Four-Mile Road. The sun up one hour, their journey through the mountains had begun.

It was early July and the foothills were matted with berry shrubs. Thorny-stemmed wild roses, intermingling with the vines of wild grapes, scented the air. The two burros, saddled with tent, bags, and utensils, plodded along the narrow, winding path, stopping frequently to feed on elderberries, currants, and strawberries.

The green leaves and needled branches of aspen and spruce laced the blue sky overhead, and Charles and Grace stopped often to look up, attracted by the flash of a tanager, the song of a bluebird, the rap of a woodpecker, the flutter of a grouse or sage hen. A porcupine darted across their path, and by the time the sun shone overhead at noon, they'd glimpsed a bobcat, a weasel, a marten, another porcupine, and dozens of rabbits.

At a brisk-flowing stream, Charles and Grace watered the burros, tying them to the branch of a tree. Charles waded out to cast for trout, and Grace sat at the water's edge, leaning against the trunk of a tree as she relaxed, watching a fleecy cloud drift across the sky.

Midstream, Charles met with quick success. Grace rose, gathered wood for the fire, and set it while Charles cleaned his catch.

The aroma of pan-fried fish filled the air as the pair cooked their meal over the open fire. They ate bountifully and shared their fare with the burros. Then they cleaned their utensils, poured water on the firebed, and were on their way.

The path wound through the foothills to the higher slopes. Here columbine grew in the shade of aspens and lichens clung to the rocks. In late afternoon they came to a meadow edged by a willow-hung stream. Spiranthes grew among the grasses and calypso and lady slippers followed the water. The burros stopped to feed, oblivious to all but the feast before them.

Laughing, Charles and Grace unsaddled their flop-eared companions and named them Jake and Dick. Here where their faithful animals could feed and water at will, they pitched their tent, basking in the beautiful setting.

They stayed several days in that meadow, following its by-paths—hiking, tracking game, and fishing. Then the pair saddled and packed the burros and the little caravan moved along again, plodding down the side of the mountain under an overcast sky. Suddenly raindrops the size of half-dollars began to fall, spattering noisily on the trees and foliage around them. Seeing an overhang farther down, the little group hurried to take shelter, huddling there until the rain stopped. But it was an on-again-off-again game the rain played that day. When it stopped, the travelers started once more, and when it started they scrambled for cover. At five o'clock the rain outsmarted them. Soaked to the skin and laughing helplessly, they continued down the canyon in the pouring rain to Jack Rabbit Lodge, where Grace had once camped with friends.

They had no idea that the little building was occupied

or that their progress down the narrow canyon was being watched from the porch by writer James Husted, who, inspired by their journey through the mountains, would welcome them and record their experiences in a chronicle called A *ROCKY MOUNTAIN IDYLL.*

Their progress through the mountains became a series of adventures taking them over the Great Divide and spanning a distance of more than two hundred miles.

During the first month they camped in a cave at Dome Rock near Howbert, waking one morning to see a magnificent four-point buck descending to water across from their shelter. Spending the remainder of that morning fishing, Charles returned to stretch under a tree with his writing pad and pencil.

"Are you writing a letter?" Grace called as she draped their creek-washed laundry over low bushes.

"No!"

"What, then?"

"Not much of anything. A limerick of sorts, I guess you'd call it," he said, tearing a sheet from his pad and folding it for his pocket.

"Charles, *let me see!*"

Grace darted over and reached into his pocket. She unfolded the paper on which he had scrawled:

THE DONKMOBILE

In this day of grease and gas and trouble,
Give me a Donkmobile packed double!
Their tires don't burst nor their engines go wrong;
You see all the scenery, each hour's an hour long.

You don't count miles, only joys of the trail;
You can walk at the head end or stroll at the tail.

Donks live on scenery and empty cans,
They eat up the scraps and lick out the pans.

There's never a detour on the road they take,
They plod over ground at the pace of a snake.
For unmatched pleasure, and fun at each meal,
Pack all your duffle on a Donkmobile!

"Charles, I *like* it! I'm sending this to Mr. Husted. I didn't know you were a poet!"

"Well, nothing's transpired to enlighten you otherwise, Grace. Now let's eat! It's lunchtime and I'm starved!"

Throughout their two-year jaunt, Charles often wrote their experiences in impromptu rhyme. These Grace included in her letters to James Husted, whose interest and pleasure in them matched her own.

Toward the end of July the pair was trudging up a hill one afternoon on their way to Leadville when a big car with Nebraska plates came along, spotted them, and stopped on the steep pitch. Two men with cameras piled out, waving to them and shouting,

"Hi-ho! Hold on a minute, there! We want to get you!"

Smiling, husband and wife were photographed, donkmobile and all.

Averaging eighteen miles a day, Charles and Grace reached Hartzel on the last day of July. There the hospitality of the ranchers compelled them to stay a week before moving on. Their walking stunt attracted friendly interest all along the way, and opened the hearts of ranch families wherever they went. Seldom could they pass a ranch without being waved in for an hour or so of conversation and coffee. Often as the pair left, bundles of fresh vegetables, fruits, and home-canned staples were pressed upon them with many wishes for a safe and happy journey.

From Hartzel they set out for Garo, where the start of a series of daily afternoon showers limited their travel to the morning hours and reduced their progress to ten or twelve miles a day.

Occasionally they would meet other campers, and six miles above Twin Bridges on the road to Weston Pass, they met a group from Cripple Creek. Charles and Grace camped with them for several days at the old Michaels place, and learned from their new friends of the excellent fishing at Black Lake, two hundred miles ahead over the Great Divide. The two decided to make Black Lake their destination. They would take a cabin in the area and make it their winter quarters. According to Charles' calculations, they would reach Black Lake by mid-autumn.

Four days later they said goodbye to their camping companions, leaving letters with them to be mailed from Cripple Creek.

Refreshed by their respite, Charles and Grace and the donkmobile covered eighteen miles in six hours, a high altitude climb which brought them to an elevation of 11,676 feet.

They rested then by a noisy creek, pitched their tent, and named the site *Wild Rose Camp* for the brilliant pink blooms that trailed throughout the area, filling the air with their fragrance. Grace gathered a few roses and put them in a letter to James Husted, saying:

". . . I only wish we could share with you all the beauties we see and enjoy each day. Please accept a few of the flowers that color and scent our days here at Wild Rose Camp."

In a postscript, Charles added,

". . . we have been lingering along the way more than we had intended—it's so hard to leave some of this spectacular scenery behind! Our mode of travel makes it possible to enjoy each view to the fullest. Were we traveling by car, we couldn't possibly see nor appreciate the scenes we come upon each day. This is an experience I wish every city man could have."

Charles and Grace and the donkmobile spent the greater part of September as ranch hands. Following a winding road high above Minturn, they had come upon a spruce grove along a lively creek and chose it as a campsite. The creek yielded magnificent trout and the surrounding woods an abundance of small game. On a two-day hunt the couple met an area rancher who, needing farmhands, asked if they might be interested in helping with the harvest.

Side by side in the weeks that followed, husband and wife mowed hay, bound sheaves, fed and watered livestock, chopped wood, and made themselves generally useful. They enjoyed a close rapport with the rancher and his family. As a side project, Charles built a fireplace for them, working at it between ranch jobs and in the evenings. Inspired by her husband's masonry, Grace carried small field rocks, mixed cement, and gave encouragement as the attractive structure took form.

Jake and Dick, the indispensable donkmobile, leisurely roamed the ranch and mingled contentedly with the other animals.

The harvesting and the fireplace completed by month's end, Charles and Grace said good-bye to their ranch friends and promised to stop by on their return trip.

It was October now, and the little caravan wound along narrow mountain trails, its pace slowed by the erratic snows of autumn. Frequently taking shelter in old deserted cabins, Charles and Grace empathized with the code of the mountain traveler, set by prospectors during the gold rush days and invariably posted on a shelf inside:

Find a can of beans here and eat
hearty. Leave a can of beans so
the next fellow can do the same.

By the first of November they had made their way over the Great Divide. Arriving at Minturn, the pair conceded at last to the snows of winter.

"We'll have to write off Black Lake, Grace," Charles laughed ruefully, "great fishing or no! It's time to settle down and make our peace with the elements."

"I'll go along with that, Charles. Gore Creek fishing is good enough for me!"

They found an unused cabin near the creek and inquired of an area ranchowner who gave them permission to make it their winter quarters. Located within the boundaries of Mann's Ranch, the sturdy loghouse, complete with a stout wood stove and a corral for the donkmobile, met their needs perfectly.

Charles and Grace and the donkmobile ended their journey none too soon. Within three weeks snow covered the Gore Mountains as far as the eye could see, ice sealed the lakes and Gore Creek, and strong winds piled drifts against their door and windows. A deep, vast stillness lay all about them, starkly white, the day sky brilliant blue in contrast.

Hired as a ranch-hand by Frank Mann, Charles left the cabin early each morning wearing heavy snowshoes and bundled in a parka against the piercing cold. Grace stayed behind keeping the fire going, sawing and splitting wood for fuel as Charles had taught her, and doing her household chores.

Charles and Grace marvelled at the timeliness of their arrival at Mann's Ranch. They knew with certainty that they had been guided to their right place. For Charles' services they received fresh milk, grain, meats, vegetables, and fruits.

The Manns were a warm and gracious family. There was a "Son of Mann," as the Patches affectionately called him, a golden-haired seven-year-old who came to their cabin regularly to check the two trap lines Charles had laid and to ride the friendly burros. A gold-and-white collie always at his side, the blue-eyed, rosy-cheeked boy made his way down the trail to the Patches' cabin often, sometimes carrying a cake or pie his mother sent along for them.

Their baby would arrive in less than two months. Charles spent his evenings now making a cradle of polished pine, and in the afternoons he and Grace took long walks in the snow. On Sundays they rode a ranch sleigh to one of the neighboring farms for an hour's conversation with friends. On their return they took a roundabout route to meet new people, make new friends.

CHAPTER XI

THE BIRTH OF DIANA

"Hi-ho! Good morning!"

Laying feed for the burros inside the corral, Charles looked up to see a sleigh coming down the road carrying the neighbors who lived higher up the mountain.

"We're going into town for supplies! Can we get you anything?" Mr. Baldauf shouted, waving and smiling as the sleigh approached the cabin.

"Good morning! Why, thanks! Maybe so. I'll check with Grace. Come on in!"

"We're all bundled up, so we'll wait here, Charles. We want to get to Minturn and back before supper!"

Inside the cabin, Grace made a list and Charles took it out to the Baldaufs. They rode off and Charles went back to feeding the burros. That done, he went inside to wash his hands at the basin. Catching his reflection in the time-stained mirror nailed above the wash-stand, he said,

"I think I'll shave, Grace."

He reached for his bowl and brush and lathered his face. Halfway through shaving he heard Grace call out,

"Charles! Charles—I—believe it's time! I think it's time for the baby—"

"All right, Grace! But tell that baby not to dare come until old Dad finishes shaving!"

Charles toweled hastily. He placed pans of water on the stove and went to Grace.

For weeks all had been in readiness. They had lined the cradle Charles had made with sheepskin, and now for added warmth they filled hot water bottles and laid them in it.

Throughout their journey they'd carried a sterile container which held the equipment needed for the baby's birth. Opening it now, Charles placed the items onto a sterile cloth. Among the purchases from Lane Bryant were hygienically-packaged linens. They unfolded these and dressed the bed.

By the time the Baldauf family returned from town that afternoon, Charles and Grace were the proud parents of a beautiful, healthy baby girl. Sitting up in bed, Grace saw the approaching sleigh through the window.

The Baldaufs were thrilled at the news.

"When we came by this morning, we had no idea your baby would be born today!" Mrs. Baldauf exclaimed.

"When you came by this morning, *we* had no idea our baby would be born today!" Charles laughed.

"But I should have been here to help! Had I only known, I never would have gone into town! Thank God everything went well!"

"Yes, everything went well, thank God."

Grateful as they were for their neighbor's well-meaning interest, the birth of their baby took place exactly as Charles and Grace had planned — the mother the nurse, the father the doctor, and the Omnipresence guiding them, directing them. Their baby had arrived easily, comfortably, peacefully; and never had they been so deeply aware of the Presence and Power of God with them as they had been in that hour.

The experience had not been without its light side. An entertaining story-teller, Charles had saved his funniest jokes for the time during delivery when Grace needed most to relax. His graphic humor left Grace unable to distinguish between laughing cramps and labor pangs. Charles' foresight brought little Diana Lightfoot Patch into the world on a peal of irrepressible laughter.

Sitting up in bed later that afternoon, Grace wrote the news of their baby's birth to her parents.

Grace Lightfoot's reply to her daughter's letter reached Charles and Grace through the Minturn Post Office eight days after Diana was born.

"Traipsing through the mountains on foot while expecting a baby! And having your baby up there—God knows where—all alone in a cabin! I don't believe it! I don't believe a word of it! Your father and I won't believe it until you send pictures of the baby so we can see for ourselves!"

"Well—back to Minturn, Grace. We'll have to send pictures!" Charles said, laughing.

Soon after the pictures reached the Lightfoots in Washington, the first of a steady stream of packages came for baby Diana. William and Grace couldn't do enough for their little granddaughter. They were thrilled with her and delighted with her name.

It was their writer friend James Husted who had influenced Charles and Grace in the naming of their baby. When they first met, he had remarked that Grace reminded him of the heroine of "Diana of the Green Van," a popular novel based on the camping experiences of a nature-loving young woman. Later he had sent them a copy of the book and they'd read it with special interest as they traveled through the mountains.

Charles and Grace had written to James Husted regularly throughout their journey. When Diana was born Charles wrote him:

> "Hail to Diana Lightfoot Patch!
> The Mountain Baby born January
>   fourteenth at Gore Creek!
> God give her joy so deep
> Not any ill can darken it
> Nor any sweet can cloy

For so alone can Life fulfill
  Itself.
God give her joy!"

At the end of their second year in the mountains, Charles sent a final letter to James Husted telling him of their plans to return to Denver:

". . . *Grace, Diana and I will retrace our steps now and make our way home. We'll stop along the way to see the friends we made on our forward journey and have them meet Baby Diana.*

"I have made solo trips to Denver during recent months, leaving Grace and Diana at the cabin on Mann's ranch, watched over by 'Shep,' a large collie. Plans are now complete for the reopening of my office in the fall. Soon the three Patches will leave these beloved mountains to become city dwellers again. After living so long in the open—with the sky for a ceiling, the mountainsides for walls, and the good earth our larder—living and working indoors will take some getting used to!

"As we head homeward we carry treasured memories of the greatest to the least of our experiences. Certainly among the former is our meeting with you in the early days of our journey and the friendship we've shared since that time. We cannot tell you how much your letters have meant to us as we've traveled through these glorious Rockies. We look forward to the time when you will visit us in Denver and meet 'The Mountain Baby.'

"A line of love from the Dianas.

Sincerely,
Charles Patch"

Their Rocky Mountain adventure ended in Cripple Creek, where it had begun. There Charles and Grace sold the two burros to a local rancher. It was not easy for them to watch *Jake* and *Dick* being led away, knowing they would never see them again. The Donkmobile had been part of their lives for two years. Charles, Grace and Diana were deeply attached to the pair. Plodding along now with their purchaser the faithful burros were a picture the Patches would remember always: their shaggy coats, gray except for their white noses and bellies; the black stripe that looped over their withers and half-way down their front legs; their scrubby manes, stiff and erect; their smooth tails with the tufted ends; their long floppy ears. They would miss hearing the Donkmobile's startling two-syllabled bray—the first shrill, the second deep and hoarse. At a distance now, the burros followed their new owner around a bend in the road and disappeared from view. Charles and Grace looked at each other. Their two-year idyll was now a memory.

Two-and-a-half hours later, the Patches arrived by train in Denver. As they walked away from the *Colorado Southern* in Union Station, the sophistication and tempo of the city loomed sharp. Charles flagged a car then and they were on their way to Monroe Street and home.

The neat square of lawn that surrounded their bungalow looked cramped and artificial to them, accustomed as they were to rugged, expansive camping areas and cabin grounds matted with shrubs and vines. Inside the house, which Charles had readied for them on his recent trips to Denver, the carpeted floors felt strange to Grace as she walked through the rooms. She came back to the living room then and sat on the sofa. Taking the chair opposite her, Charles lifted Diana onto his lap. They had crossed the threshold of their former world and were home again in Denver.

The next Sunday the Patches got into their Ford and drove to the newly-located Divine Science Church at Fourteenth and Williams Street. The new church had been built while they were living in the mountains. It rose before them now, a large, magnificent structure styled in classic Greek architecture, breath-taking in its beauty. It bore rich testimony to the growth of Divine Science in Denver.

The second Sunday in September announcement was made from the pulpit that Divine Science class instruction would begin in October. After the service, Grace looked over the list of courses and enrolled in Mrs. Nelson's Bible Class. Later she would study Spiritual Psychology with Dr. Brooks, then take the course in Consecration taught by Anna L. Palmer. The prospect of further study was exciting to Grace. Divine Science was her element. She was glad to be in it again.

As Charles and Grace adjusted once more to city living their days became filled with activity. Their friends were eager to see them and they visited and were visited. On a Sunday in October James Husted drove to Denver from his home in Pueblo to meet "The Mountain Baby." The writer and baby Diana were enchanted with each other and spent a delightful afternoon together. During his visit Mr. Husted surprised Charles and Grace with the gift of a handbound volume titled *A ROCKY MOUNTAIN IDYLL*. It contained the substance of the letters in journal form that he had received from the Patches during their two-year adventure in the mountains.

Three weeks later the little book traveled with Grace and Diana to Washington, D.C., on a four-day visit made to introduce William and Grace Lightfoot to their little granddaughter.

Charles had reopened his office immediately after their return to Denver. He placed notice of his resumed practice in *The Denver Post*. Calls for appointments came in sporadically. Charles maintained his office hours confident that, as his return became known, more and more of his patients would contact him.

But the response, slow from the start, slackened. Within five months it became apparent that the greater number of his patients would not again seek his services.

Income that first year was meager. The second year showed little increase. Charles and Grace found themselves having to draw on their savings to meet their needs. By the third year their bank account had dwindled alarmingly. To offset their losses they gave up their home on Monroe Street and moved into a small furnished apartment on Sherman Avenue.

Charles brooded about his shrunken practice. Blank page after blank page in his appointment book represented idle hours, unproductive days.

Discouragement set in, then anxiety. Deeply troubled, he struggled to meet the needs of his family. Nervousness brought on intense migraine headaches and their severity progressed to the point that often he could not function effectively in his office. Unable to receive his patients at these times, he had Grace make cancellations. Aware of this further damage to his practice, Charles became ridden with self-reproach. Finally, his faith in himself was totally shaken. Seriously ill now, he gave up his practice entirely.

They lived meagerly for several months on the little money that was left. Then they had none at all. Struggling to control her panic, Grace wrote to her father asking for help. She watched the return mail anxiously. When it came, his reply left her shocked and hurt.

"I won't give you a single nickel," her father wrote Grace. "You got yourselves into this, now get yourselves out of it. And let it be a lesson to both of you."

Disbelief and terror washed over Grace. Charles needed medical attention that they could not afford. Weak, and able to eat or drink very little, Charles kept to his bed now. Grace herself was exhausted from lack of sleep and worry. It was all she could do to take care of Charles and look after little Diana. As she stared now at the nearly empty icebox, a knock came at the door. It was their landlord, come to remind

Grace that they were behind in their rent. Payment would have to be made immediately.

Fighting to control her panic, Grace left Diana with Charles the next morning and went downtown to the YWCA. There she explained her need and applied for emergency employment. The interviewer looked over Grace's qualifications and offered her a job in a dental factory, available immediately. Although the job paid a shockingly low wage, at least it would provide food and milk for their child. Grace accepted it.

The work was arduous and required long hours of standing at a plaster bench running up impressions and mounting models on an articulator. After a week on her feet in this restricting position Grace suffered severe backaches and tensed neck muscles.

Shocked to find that her first paycheck would not meet even their basic needs of food and rent, Grace went to her employer immediately and explained her need for a raise. He agreed to an increase and during the next two weeks Grace worked less mindful of her stiffness and soreness. The wage supplement, she reminded herself frequently, would compensate for the physical pain and discomfort she had to endure.

She received her second paycheck and with it a second shock. She'd been given a raise of only fifty cents. Certain that an error had been made, she went to her employer.

"Mr. Schneider, there's been a mistake. My check shows a raise of only fifty cents."

"My dear Mrs. Patch, there is no mistake," Mr. Schneider stated. "That's our rate of increase here."

Stunned, and unable to reply, Grace walked from the office and out of the factory. She fought to hold back the tears as she walked homeward. Finding it impossible to go on, she cut through the park and sat down on a bench. The tears flowed unchecked now. In spite of them she made a concentrated effort to think things through. *"Dear Father in Heaven, please help me!"* She cried within herself. *"Something has got to be done! Things cannot go on like this any longer!"*

"Prayer," Dr. Nona Brooks had stated again and again from the pulpit, *"never fails. And the prayer that never fails is right thinking and right living! Prayer changes things. Prayer causes things to happen quite differently from the way they would happen had not the prayer been made. Turn from your problem to the Presence. Stop feeding the difficulty with your attention. Give your attention to God, the Presence of All Good! In the face of any difficulty, remain God-centered—Good-centered—and soon you will find yourself safely out of the trouble."*

The tears stopped. Her mind cleared. She straightened. *What in the world was she doing in that factory laboring for a pittance in the first place? Had she forgotten that she had both college and nurses' training and was equipped to perform skilled services at a much higher rate of pay?* In her panic she had grabbed at any straw. She knew now what she should do. She would contact the University of Colorado and ask to be interviewed for a position in keeping with her qualifications. Gaining courage and peace from her decision, she rose and walked home.

She began making inquiries early the next morning. Finding that the University of Colorado's medical school had relocated in Denver, Grace took the streetcar across town and met with the professor of Physiology, Dr. Steele. Learning of her circumstances, Dr. Steele said kindly,

"I don't have an opening in my office, Mrs. Patch. But I know someone who does. Come with me. We'll see Dr. Lewis. Do you remember him?"

"Yes. Dr. Lewis was my Biochemistry teacher at Boulder."

They entered Dr. Lewis' office farther down the hall, and Dr. Steele said,

"Dr. Lewis, this is Mrs. Grace Lightfoot Patch, a former student of yours. Mrs. Patch is interested in a position here. I suggested she talk with you."

"Good afternoon, Mrs. Patch. Yes, I remember you. Please sit down," Dr. Lewis responded cordially.

Dr. Steele left them then, and Dr. Lewis said,

"So you would like to work here at the medical school?"

"Yes." For the second time that morning, Grace described the crisis in her home.

"Well, now," Dr. Lewis said briskly, "let's see what can be done about all this." He walked across the room to a cabinet and thumbed through a drawer.

"Your record should be right here, Mrs. Patch. Let me see. *Lightfoot, Grace E.* Yes. Here it is," he said, pulling out her folder. He studied its contents, then looked at Grace and said,

"This is a coincidence, Mrs. Patch. This morning a young woman came in to apply for this job who has an excellent background in typing and shorthand, but knows nothing about chemistry. Now you've come along, knowing chemistry and other sciences, but with no background in typing or shorthand! Now then, Mrs. Patch. If you are willing to learn typing and shorthand, I'll give *you* the job."

"Oh, I *am*! I'm perfectly willing to learn them."

Dr. Robert Lewis hired Grace right away. Giving her a month's salary in advance, he placed her on a half-day schedule for which she received full day's pay. Grace immediately enrolled in the afternoon program at the Denver Opportunity School to learn typing and shorthand.

Her world brightened. Grace was on familiar ground now, doing work that was interesting and pleasant. And she was earning an excellent salary. As Dr. Lewis' assistant her job was a responsible one. She had complete charge of his laboratory, office records, student equipment, and the white rats used by students of nutrition in their experimental projects.

These little animals were kept on the top floor of the building in a room with large windows. Grace was responsible for delivering the white rats to the students in the laboratory each morning and returning them to their cages at the end of the day. Going to the cage room at the close of classes one afternoon, Grace found that she had forgotten to pull the front window shade. Strong sunlight poured into the cage of a mother rat and her litter. Conscience-stricken, Grace rushed to the window and lowered the shade. Then she hurried back to the affected cage and what she saw there made an impression that would stay with her forever. The mother rat had taken straw from the floor of the cage and had woven it among the wires of the cagefront, forming a screen to shield her babies from the burning rays of the sun.

As time went by the Patches' circumstances righted themselves. Responsible for Diana's care during the day while Grace worked, Charles willed himself to his feet. Little by little his health improved. Within six months he recovered fully. He and Grace were able to discuss his illness objectively then. They reasoned that, in blaming himself for their financial failure, Charles had broken down first psychologically, then physically. As they talked together, Grace was able to pinpoint the cause of her husband's periodic withdrawal from the routine and pressures of his profession.

Charles had not wanted to become a dentist. But when he was young his parents nonetheless urged him to go into dentistry and put him through Harvard. After he came west and began studying Divine Science, Charles felt that he would have to give up dentistry. He believed he couldn't follow its Truth Principle if he were being constantly confronted with the appearance of disease and decay. Finally he resolved this inner conflict, reasoning that, since he had a specialized skill which could bring comfort and healing to his fellowman, it would be wasteful not to use it. But, if he had it to do over, he told Grace, he would have become a forest ranger, or game warden, or guide, working entirely out-of-doors.

Listening as Charles talked, Grace gratefully observed his regained strength and confidence and reflected on the occasion which had brought about his healing. Throughout the years, it was their custom to have Dr. Nona Brooks as their New Year's Day guest. Again as the new year approached, Grace had invited their minister to have dinner with them, certain that Dr. Brooks' presence would comfort her ill husband. The light that came into their home with Dr. Brooks that day stayed with them. Embracing them both, she stated firmly:

"*Now*, children, is the time to give your attention to Truth, to Principle, to the Omnipresence. Be not problem-centered, but Principle-centered! Turn now from the appearance and hold fast to Truth. Behold your Good. Omnipresence—God with you! Good with you! Now is the time for you to affirm that God is All, God is Everywhere, God is here. God is here as your Abundant Supply. Affirm that abundance, affirm that supply. God is here as perfect Health and Healing. Affirm that health, affirm that healing. It is your Divine Birthright. Go forth now and claim that which is rightfully yours as children of God—Omnipresent Abundance, Supply, Health, Healing; Omnipresent Good in you and with you!"

Their financial affairs stabilized. With the return of Charles' health, Grace enrolled again in the Divine Science classes at the church. Nona Brooks was her teacher now. Under Dr. Brooks' guidance, Grace advanced steadily in her understanding of Truth.

Joining practice with an established Denver dentist, Charles resumed the responsibility of supporting his family and Grace gave up her job at the medical school.

Throughout their ordeal Grace hd corresponded regularly with her mother. But it was not until she had begun studying Truth again that she was able to forgive her father for the rejecting letter he had written her when her husband had been ill.

Happy about the improvement in Charles' and Grace's lives and that it was no longer necessary for her daughter to work, Grace Lightfoot begged them to come to Washington so that she and William could see their little granddaughter again.

"Mother, it will be several years before we will be able to afford even a short vacation," Grace wrote in reply. *"But why don't you and Papa come to Denver to visit us? We'd love to have you and the trip would do you good."*

"No, Gracie. I won't come to Denver. I can't. That's where Fairy died. I'll never come back to Denver again. Never." Grace Lightfoot answered.

When Grace told Charles about her mother's response, he persuaded her to travel to Washington with Diana to see her parents. Two weeks later, Charles saw his wife and daughter off at Union Station.

Talking with her daughter on their first afternoon together, Grace Lightfoot apologized again for the cruel letter William had written her during their crisis.

"Your father's insensitive stand made me very unhappy. I hope you have forgiven him, Gracie."

"Yes, I've forgiven him, Mama. Really I have. Actually, it was the best thing he could have done, I came to realize later. It threw me on my own resources and made me see that I could meet and master any situation. I learned to take care of myself, and gained a great deal of confidence as a result. I'll never be afraid of anything again."

CHAPTER XII

BY MUTUAL AGREEMENT

America rode the crest of a wave of prosperity when Herbert Hoover took office as President in 1929. The new President proclaimed to his people,

". . . . . . . we shall soon be in sight of the day when poverty will be banished from this nation."

Yet seven months later the country fell victim to the tragic October stock market crash that signalled the start of The Great Depression. There followed an extensive economic breakdown. Credit tightened; trade fell off. Widespread bank failures swept away the savings of people everywhere and mortgage foreclosures claimed the businesses and homes of thousands.

In Denver, the practice Charles Patch had worked to rebuild dwindled as patients, unable to afford treatment, cancelled appointments; forfeited dental care; failed to pay for services rendered. Again in financial crisis, Charles became increasingly tense, anxious. Yet throughout, Grace chose to remain true to her understanding of Omnipresence, Truth. Mindful of Truth's healing influence in their lives, she had continued year after year in earnest study. During her long, close association with Nona Brooks there took place a transfer of spirit from teacher to student that enabled Grace to live the Truth that had been revealed to her. In recognition of her dedication to the Truth Principle and her consecration to the Healing Consciousness, the Denver Divine

Science Church licensed her as a practitioner. Grace opened an office in downtown Denver which she shared with another practitioner, maintaining Tuesday and Thursday hours that coincided with Diana's school schedule. Offering her time in healing service, she received all who came: the poor, the ill, the handicapped, the troubled, the discouraged.

An impoverished America still struggled against a deepening depression three years later when Grace received word from her mother in Washington that her father, ill for a short time, had died. Leaving Diana in the care of her friend Sybil Hosmer Spear, Grace left immediately for the east.

After the funeral her mother asked Grace to stay with her for a time to help her in her adjustment. Grace remained in Washington a month. At the end of that time she urged her mother to give up her property in Washington and return with her to Denver.

"I've told you before, Gracie. I will *never* go back to Denver. *Never*," Grace Lightfoot stated firmly. "Washington is my home now. I will stay here."

"All right, Mama. But how will you manage alone?"

"I'll be all right. Gracie — times are hard, and things are so awful everywhere — how are you and Charles doing? Is he making enough for you to get along?"

Her daughter made no reply.

"I see. The answer is *no*. Isn't that so, Gracie? Now look here. There's plenty of room in this house. Why don't all of you come here to live with me? Gracie, if there's any money to be made, it's here in Washington. I'm sure Charles could get established in this area. It would make it easier for all of us — we could all be together."

Perhaps this was the answer. Charles' practice yielded little — less than enough to keep them going. Discouraged, Charles was nervous, dejected. It placed a strain on their relationship.

A fresh start. Yes. A fresh start could be the answer.

She wrote to Charles that evening, urging him to consider coming to Washington to start a new practice. Here they could live comfortably in her mother's home. Here, together, they could make a new beginning.

The prospect of a more rewarding practice in the east appealed to Charles and lifted his spirits. As soon as he could settle his affairs in Denver, he wrote Grace in reply, he and Diana would come to Washington.

Grace was filled with fresh hope at Charles' response. She knew she had taken the right step. She wrote next to her associate practitioner, telling her of their new plans, and requesting that her patients be assigned to another practitioner.

She would not be returning to Denver! Grace gazed at her pen now, amazed at the courage with which she had written the words. Yet she had been prepared for this moment, this announcement, well in advance of her arrival in Washington.

In Denver, Grace had always driven Charles to work. On the way home she would ride to Cheesman Park for an early morning meditation. Cheesman Park was her favorite place. It afforded a breath-taking view of Mt. Evans, which rose between Long's Peak and Pike's Peak. Standing alone at sunrise before those great mountains one morning two weeks before her father's death, the feeling came over her that soon she would move from Denver, that soon she would live in the east. Attempting to cope with the impartation, she was overcome by sadness at the thought of moving from the west and leaving her beloved mountains behind. How could she live without seeing them at sunrise, at sunset each day! It seemed more than she could bear. Tears filled her eyes. The scene blurred before her and she stood weighted by the heaviness of her heart.

"Grace. What you love and adore in us is not out here but within you. We live within you in the love that you feel for

*us in your heart. Wherever you go, we will be with you.
Wherever you go, you will carry us with you in your heart."*

Beautiful Mt. Evans had spoken to her. In that moment
courage welled up within her, flowing to her from her beloved
mountains. With it came peace. In that peace was the
assurance that now she could go anywhere, live any place on
earth and be perfectly content.

Now, happy at the prospect of their new life together, a
buoyant, smiling Grace met Charles and Diana at Washington's Union Station. They were together again, a family
complete.

During the next three weeks Charles searched the Washington area hoping to find a solid opportunity for his practice. He found nothing. Day by day his disappointment
mounted. By the month's end Charles was discouraged. He
talked of going to Boston. He knew people there. He was
licensed to practice in Boston. He felt he could be successful
there. He urged Grace to consider Boston, where they could
become financially secure.

But something within Grace held back. She did not want
to go. She remained unpersuaded, choosing to stay in Washington. Finally she faced the fact that events of recent years
had climaxed, causing a change in their relationship. Grace
realized now as did Charles that something had gone from
their marriage. In tacit hope that the situation would resolve
itself, Grace said nothing. Nor did Charles. They agreed at
last that she and Diana would stay on at her mother's home,
and that he would go to Boston alone. Once established
there, he would send for them.

As she saw her husband off at Union Station, Grace knew
that her twelve-year marriage to Charles Patch had ended.
With that realization came peace. Charles would be all right.
She and Diana would be all right. She held firmly to her
awareness of the Presence of God, Truth, in them and with

them as they moved forward independently of each other. All would be well with them. Her faith was strong.

In her new setting, her new circumstances, Grace thought often of Denver — her friends there, her Divine Science teachers, her practitioner work, her minister Dr. Nona Brooks, her church. *Her church!* She had committed herself to staying in Washington. *But she could not do without her church.* She could forego all that had made up her life in Denver, *but she could not live without her church!* She would locate a Divine Science Church in this city and begin attending with Diana right away. She checked the church listings in the weekend papers. There was no Divine Science listing. *No Divine Science Church in Washington!* Disbelief mingled with disappointment within her as she attempted to come to terms with the situation. She thought of Dr. James Edgerton, who she knew lived in nearby Arlington, Virginia. Dr. Edgerton was President of the International New Thought Alliance, an organization of churches and centers that followed the Principle of Omnipresence, Truth. Grace had heard James Edgerton speak from the Denver pulpit. She would telephone him. Possibly he could direct her to a Washington New Thought church or center.

"Come over to the house tomorrow afternoon and spend some time with us," Dr. Edgerton invited her on the telephone. "We'll have a good talk together."

In her conversation with Dr. and Mrs. Edgerton, Grace learned that there was no New Thought church in Washington. She was incredulous.

"Well, there certainly *ought* to be!" she exclaimed. "Oh! I don't know how in the world I'll manage without my church!"

The three of them sat silent for a time, thinking over the situation.

"Dr. Edgerton," Grace said at length, "if you will start a

Divine Science group here, I'll back you one-hundred per-
cent. If you would head a group, I'd help in every way that
I could."

"No *indeed!* I wouldn't *think* of it!" James Edgerton
laughed, shaking his head. "Every teacher who's tried it in this
area has failed. New Thought doesn't stand a chance in
Washington, Grace. This town is too transient. New Thought
doesn't stand a chance."

"But *something* should be available — at least *something,*"
Grace persisted.

"Well now, there are one or two practitioners in town, and
maybe a few home study groups that meet here and there.
But that's all. I can give you the name of a fine practitioner
that I know personally — Miss Emma Gray. I'm sure you
would enjoy meeting her."

Grace telephoned Miss Emma Gray the next day and made
an appointment to meet with her the following Sunday afternoon. The venerable Miss Gray welcomed Grace warmly and
graciously. The hour of conversation that followed became
the basis of a valued friendship between the two like-minded
women. A practitioner-teacher of the Truth Principle, Emma
Gray welcomed all who were interested in studying Truth and
all who were in need of healing through spiritual treatment.
She received her students and patients privately, by appointment only. Therefore Miss Gray raised her eyebrows question-
ingly when a knock came at her door as she and Grace sat
talking on a later Sunday. One of her students had been passing by and, troubled about a matter, felt the need of a prayer
treatment. Inviting her to come in, Miss Gray introduced
Grace to Mathilde Rochon, a young woman who later would
become Grace's closest friend.

Mathilde Rochon was Catholic in background, Grace
learned. Some time ago, she had come upon some Truth
literature and, convinced that its philosophy represented an

intelligent approach to life, she had come to Emma Gray for private instruction in Truth. After a glimpse of "the higher way," as Mathilde called it, she had accepted Miss Gray's teaching of the Truth Principle, Omnipresence. "Completely and without reservation! So here I am!" Mathilde said happily.

Grace and Mathilde left Miss Gray's apartment at the same time that afternoon. As they walked down the steps together, Mathilde said, "Emma Gray has a powerful consciousness, Grace. I've had several healings as a result of her treatments. She's up in years now, though, and sometimes when I go to her for help, she'll fall asleep right in the middle of a treatment! But—when she wakes up, the work is done! The healing follows! Now *that's* consciousness!"

They laughed, and Grace said, "She's *marvelous*. I'm very fond of her; and very grateful to her. It means a great deal to me to be able to talk with someone who knows and lives Truth. I'm from Denver. I studied Truth there for several years. I miss my friends in the teaching there."

"Oh? Grace, listen—I'm going to Florence Willard Day's class next Thursday afternoon at two. Would you like to go along?"

"What kind of class is it?"

"It's a New Thought Study Group. Mrs. Day is an outstanding teacher. You would like her—and you'd have an opportunity to meet people—wonderful people who share your interest in Truth."

Grace went to class with Mathilde the following Thursday and felt an instant rapport with Mrs. Florence Willard Day. Mrs. Day conducted her class on a reading-discussion basis. Her presentation of Truth was inspiring. Although it was not quite like Divine Science which she had studied in Denver, Grace nonetheless came away uplifted in consciousness.

One evening a few weeks later, Florence Willard Day telephoned Grace at her mother's home. "Grace," she said, "I'm
going to the National Penwomen's Convention next week and
won't be able to meet with my Thursday group. Would you
be willing to lead the class that day so that it can go on as
usual?"

"Oh — well — I've never done anything like that before, Mrs.
Day. But — yes, I'd be glad to try. I'll do my best."

"I have confidence in you, Grace. You'll do very well. In
my apartment at two then next Thursday afternoon. I'll leave
my key with the clerk at the desk. Thank you, Grace."

In Mrs. Day's apartment the next Thursday Grace received
the six-member group and explained their leader's absence.
Then she told the group a little about herself and her Divine
Science background, and answered their questions about the
Denver Church and its minister, Dr. Nona L. Brooks, of
whom one or two of them had heard. Pleased at their interest,
Grace gave them an account of the growth of the Divine
Science movement in Denver under the leadership of its co-
founder, Dr. Brooks. As Grace described the courses offered
in the church's college, the group grew more and more interested. The two hours passed swiftly. The meeting had been
a success.

Mrs. Day's meetings notwithstanding, Grace continued to
long for the Divine Science Church — for Divine Science fellowship and worship in Washington. Finally she persuaded
her mother to let her hold small meetings in her home and
ran a two-line ad in the *Washington Post* offering a Monday
noon healing service.

At the close of her noon service one day, Grace was taken
aside by Carol and Jimmy Bost and two others whom she had
met at Florence Willard Day's Thursday sessions.

"Florence Willard Day passed away two weeks ago," Jimmy
Bost told Grace. "We need someone to take over the leader-

ship of our group. We'd like to have you. Would you consider it?"

Grace thought about it for several minutes. Then she said, "I'd be glad to—*if* you would be willing to study *Divine Science*, and if you would be willing to call yourselves *Divine Scientists*."

Grace withdrew as the group discussed among themselves the study of Truth as presented by Divine Science.

It made no difference to them, they decided. What Grace had shared with them in Mrs. Day's absence that Thursday afternoon was precisely what they believed, precisely what they were studying anyway. Yes. They were willing to study Divine Science, and they were willing to call themselves Divine Scientists. Going to Grace with their decision, the group talked on the porch with their new teacher, and there in full sunlight they had their first meditation together.

As she met with her group weekly at midday, Grace discovered that Washington's summers were hot—*very* hot. She agreed with her students to change their meeting time to Sunday mornings at seven.

"Why don't we have breakfast in the park, then?" Jimmy Bost suggested. Each Sunday after, they met on the porch of Grace's mother's home and went on to Rock Creek Park. They breakfasted on melon, bacon, eggs, rolls, and coffee; then had their lesson in the shade of the trees. Well ahead of the heat, they were home by ten o'clock.

Grace's students were enthusiastic. They brought friends to the early morning meetings and soon their number doubled. Observing their interest and regular attendance, Grace offered them a course in *Basic Principles of Truth*. For this, with her mother's permission, they met in the living room of her home.

Grace Lightfoot busied herself with errands or reading each Tuesday afternoon, politely refusing her daughter's invitation to join her group. Occasionally she went off to a church function, staunch Methodist that she was, or to a meeting of the *DAR*. She had become a member of the *DAR* during her early years in Washington.

"Soon after your father and I were settled here I went down to the National Archives and began my genealogical research," she had told her daughter proudly. "I traced our lineage to *Jesse Foote*, my maternal great-grandfather, who served in the Lexington alarm from Colchester, Connecticut, in April, 1775, under Captain Eliphalet Bulkley, and also under Captain Horton in Colonel Jeduthan Baldwin's regiment."

Proof at last of this ancestral link had fulfilled Grace Lightfoot's long pursued plan for membership in The Society of the Daughters of the American Revolution, a group formed in the late 1800's to honor the memory of ancestors who fought in the Revolutionary War.

In September Grace Lightfoot told the younger Grace, "My dear, I'll be entertaining my Judge Lynne Chapter here next Tuesday. Please postpone your meeting until the following week. I'll need the house to myself that day."

"Oh—certainly—I understand, Mother. But I wish I had known earlier. I could have told my class about it when we met today. I don't know if I'll be able to contact all of them. I'll try."

"Well, in that case, just go ahead and have your class as usual next Tuesday. But have them out by three o'clock. I'll need time to prepare for my dinner guests. You and your *classes*, Gracie! How in the world did you get mixed up in this crazy new religion in the first place? *Morning meditations! Afternoon classes!* I think you've lost your mind!"

Students came Tuesdays in increasing numbers. Grace Lightfoot's tolerance turned to disapproval.

"From what you've told me about this new-fangled religion of yours, Gracie, it doesn't make any sense *at all*! It smacks of sacrilege, in my opinion. How in the world can you abandon all that you were taught from childhood for this *nonsense*? I don't know what's gotten into you, Gracie. You've *changed*."

Mathilde Rochon read the situation and came forward with a solution.

"Grace, in fairness to your mother, let's admit that it is an imposition to take over her living room every Tuesday—even more so as the group grows larger. Now look here. I live alone and I have my own home. Why don't we meet at my house?"

Grace accepted Mathilde's generous offer. The group relocated and continued to grow steadily. Each week Grace carried her supply of Divine Science and other metaphysical books and periodicals to Mathilde's home. These were available to the group after class for borrowing. Afterward Grace boxed the books and took them home.

Grace returned from her class one Tuesday afternoon to find a letter from Charles in the mail. She read its contents carefully. He had opened a new office and was now practicing in a good section of Boston. He wanted her and Diana to join him as soon as possible. He missed them both very much.

Grace read the letter once more, then returned it to its envelope. She sat quietly for a time and then the certainty of what to do came to her. She would go to Boston with Diana for a few days. They would leave next Tuesday, right after her class. They would return Saturday, in time for her Sunday morning service.

On their second day together in Boston, Charles, Grace, and Diana motored north to New Hampshire. There, surrounded by stately woodlands and high green hills, they canoed on beautiful Scobie Lake. Gliding over its clear blue depths, Charles and Grace quietly discussed the state of their marriage.

"I failed you miserably as a provider," Charles stated frankly, "and I deeply regret the anguish you frequently endured as a result." With his direct gaze Charles continued, "You look wonderfully well and happy, Grace. Washington has been good for you."

They sat silent for a time, watching ten-year-old Diana trailing her hand in the water at the opposite end of the canoe. Then Grace told Charles of her Divine Science work in Washington.

"I admire all that you are doing," Charles said at length. "You took hold of Truth long ago and have moved upward into the higher work. I — envy your ability to do this. You've left me far behind, Grace."

Without bitterness, without recrimination of any kind, they agreed that their paths had diverged. It was time to go their separate ways. They had fulfilled their need for each other. They made the decision that Grace should apply for a "mutual agreement" divorce in Washington, and that Diana would live there with her.

CHAPTER XIII

DIVINE SCIENCE IN WASHINGTION, D.C.

With the onset of autumn the group that met for Sunday services in Rock Creek Park realized that soon cold weather would send them indoors for the winter. They had accomplished much since their first outdoor meeting. They had established a regular Sunday service, and were well into their first course of Divine Science study, *Basic Principles of Truth*.

The group's collection of books and periodicals had grown considerably. Students often donated metaphysical books and magazines for general use, causing the box Grace transported each week to grow heavier and heavier.

"Grace, instead of moving the books back and forth, why don't you leave them here? It would be much easier for you," Mathilde suggested after class one day.

"I *could* leave them here—but I use many of them for reference material when I make up my lessons. I'd be lost without them. Still, I could choose some to take with me. If you don't mind shelving the others, it *would* be a help. Thanks, Mathilde."

Watching Grace remove books from the box, Mathilde said, "Grace, this back and forth business is a nuisance! Now look. This is a big house. There's plenty of room here. Why don't you and Diana move in with me? The two of you would have a room of your own and complete privacy. You'd have the whole place to yourselves most of the time while I'm at work. Think about it, Grace. You're perfectly welcome to live here. I'd love to have the two of you."

"Thank you, Mathilde—how good of you. But I have Mother to consider. She'd be all alone then. Still, I don't suppose she'd mind much," Grace said, laughing. "Mother's about as independent as they come! Actually, she manages perfectly well on her own, and lets me know it!"

Grace knotted the cord she used for carrying the box and put on her sweater.

"But, you know—it would be nice not to have to listen to Mother complain about the calls that come in concerning Divine Science, and about the people who come by for counselling and treatment."

"Well—here's your freedom, Grace. You know you're welcome. I believe you and Diana would be very comfortable here. Think about it."

Later that week, Grace mentioned Mathilde's offer to her mother.

"No, I don't mind, Gracie. I don't mind at all, if that's what you want to do," her mother told her. "I do mind, though, that you've gotten yourself mixed up in this crazy new religion! And *now you're teaching it!* It's *wrong*, Gracie. *Wrong!* That's all I have to say about it."

Grace moved into Mathilde's home with Diana and promptly changed the address and phone listing in her *Washington Post* ad. The move was a step in the right direction. Now she approached her work with a sense of complete freedom and peace, and watched with gratitude as her students grew in their understanding and awareness of Truth.

One Saturday as Mathilde, Grace, and Diana were cleaning the house, a call came for Grace from the secretary of the National Penwomen's Club. As a tribute to Florence Willard Day, the club members were offering the use of their studio to the group formerly led by Mrs. Day. The studio was in the centrally-located Stoneleigh Court Hotel.

Grace and Mathilde were overwhelmed by this gracious gesture. At the service in the park the next morning, Grace's students were thrilled to learn of the Penwomen's offer. Now they could have an indoor Sunday service as well as their Tuesday class continuing at Mathilde's.

To inform the public, Grace added the new address for Sunday services to her *Washington Post* ad. She was amazed at the way the work was unfolding. What Spirit had initiated, Spirit was obviously carrying through. Her dream of Divine Science in Washington was being fulfilled.

The Penwomen's studio in the Stoneleigh Court Hotel was spacious and beautifully furnished with rich carpeting, handsome period furniture, and magnificent oil paintings. Grace inspected the studio with Mr. Barnes, the hotel manager, as she prepared for her first Sunday service there. Mr. Barnes smiled appreciatively at Grace's pleasure in the attractiveness of the room. A speaker's stand would be placed at the front of the room before her arrival Sunday mornings, he told Grace. Folding chairs in the number she specified would be set up. A nominal weekly fee of three dollars was required for the use of these extra items.

They walked to the lobby then. As she said goodbye, Grace shook Mr. Barnes' hand. At that moment a messenger boy strode through the entrance and to the desk.

"Western Union," he announced briskly. "Telegram for Mrs. Grace L. Patch."

"Oh! I'm Mrs. Patch," Grace said, surprised.

She signed quickly and opened the square of yellow paper.

The telegram was from Dr. Harvey Hardman, the new minister assigned to the Denver Divine Science Church following Dr. Nona Brooks' retirement:

"Dear Mrs. Patch,
   The Divine Science Church and College of Denver congratulates you on the success of your work in Washington stop

Our thoughts and love are with you as you conduct your first Divine Science Church service stop Rich blessings and all good wishes stop

Sincerely,

Harvey Hardman"

Grace arrived at the studio very early the next morning. Going straight to the speaker's stand, she placed Dr. Hardman's telegram in the upper right corner where she could see it during the service and draw courage from its words. She walked about then, opening windows and checking to make sure that all was in order. Satisfied, she sat down to be alone with her thoughts.

Suddenly she was overcome by a sense of inadequacy. She had experienced the feeling on occasion in the past and it terrified her now.

"Oh!" she thought. *"Washington is full of great and important people! What if one of them—or some of them—should come here today? What makes me think I have something to say that would interest any of them? Why, if a diplomat or statesman should appear, I'd fall through the floor!"* Panic gripped her. *"Oh! What am I doing here? What—why am I here?"*

All at once there came total peace. It swept away all of her fear, all her self-doubt. Truth! Omnipresence! Right here, right now, always, she was in the Presence of God, the Presence of All Good. How then could she possibly fear the presence of another person? Omnipresence! Truth! That's why she was here. That's why her teacher, Nona Brooks, had been in Denver—and why Dr. Brooks was traveling right now throughout the country and abroad, helping to establish Divine Science centers such as this all over the world.

She continued serene, thinking back over her years of Divine Science study in Denver. She recalled the faces—and

the faith—of her teachers. Jessie Bromfield. Anna L. Palmer.
Agnes Lawson. Josephine Preston. The incomparable Nona
L. Brooks. She thought of Mrs. Ernst, the practitioner whose
office she'd shared in downtown Denver. Omnipresence.
Truth. That's why she was here. Seemingly, everything had
worked together in her life to bring her to this time, this
place. The call from her mother that had brought her to
Washington; her visit with the Edgertons; her meetings with
Emma Gray; Mathilde Rochon; Florence Willard Day; Florence Day's telephone call, asking her to substitute in her
absence; the Monday noon healing meditations; the Sunday
morning services in Rock Creek Park; the group that came
to her after Mrs. Day's death, asking her to lead them; her
Tuesday class in Basic Principles.

All of this she interpreted now as an activity of consciousness. Certainly she was in her right place then, doing
the right thing. She felt an inner assurance now, strong confidence that all who came here would come because they were
drawn to Truth—drawn to Truth by an activity of consciousness, as she herself had been. She dedicated herself in that
moment to faithfully teach the Truth to all who would listen.

Grace glanced at her watch. It was ten-forty. She rose from
her chair and walked across the room to stand by the door
in welcome. Five minutes passed. There was movement in the
hallway. Two people were walking toward her. Her work had
begun.

CHAPTER XIV

A CALL FROM A FORMER PATIENT

The first time Ray Faus walked into Grace's practitioner's office in Denver he took the chair she offered him and said challengingly,

"Mrs. Patch, I'm the worst patient you ever had."

"Oh, no you're not. You're the *very best*!" was her reply.

He poured out his story. A stocks and bonds salesman, he had lost his job when the depression struck. Unable to find work, he had been without income for months. His savings were depleted. He'd lost his wife. He had a young son who meant everything to him and who was being cared for by the boy's grandmother. Ray's relationship with the child's grandmother — his mother — had deteriorated. She was a fine woman, but she preached to him continually about his drinking. He saw no real purpose to life, no real reason for his existence. Approached from any angle, life was a losing proposition. Observing people and conditions, he saw the majority as a struggling, pitiable lot. For a long time now he had been drinking heavily. To satisfy his mother, he had finally agreed to talk with her minister, Dr. Hardman of the Divine Science Church. The minister, an all right fellow, had recommended weekly consultations with a church practitioner, and had given him Grace's name and office number.

"So here I am, Mrs. Patch. But I can tell you I'm hopeless."

Before Ray Faus left Grace's office that day, he agreed to return the following week. At their next meeting, Ray stated that the need for alcohol had lessened. His mother had stopped harassing him about his drinking. During still another visit to Grace's office, Ray admitted to a better perspective through the clear eyes of sobriety. Things in general had improved. Maybe it wasn't the cards, he reasoned, but the way he played them that could make a difference. He would keep trying.

When Grace left Denver for Washington, Ray was assigned to another practitioner. Although some of her former patients wrote to her occasionally, she had not heard from Ray Faus. Now, nearly two years later, she was surprised to hear his voice on the telephone.

"Grace, I'm in New York. I traveled for a month through the midwest looking for work. No luck. So I decided to head east. No luck here, either. I'm going back to Denver. Before I go I'd like to come down to Washington to see you. I called your mother's home and she gave me your telephone number. I want you to know that you were a great help to me, Grace. I'm doing all right now."

"I'm glad to hear that, Ray. And do come down. It will be wonderful to see you again."

Two days later, Ray Faus came to Washington and visited in the afternoon with Grace at Mathilde's home. Ray was shocked to learn of Grace's separation from her husband. Noting her reticence, he turned the conversation to himself.

"Grace, I don't know what to do. There's not a job to be had that'll pay a decent wage. If I could just get steady work, and a home of my own, I could raise my boy myself. That's all I want out of life. I checked into the YMCA this morning. I think I'll look around Washington while I'm here."

When Ray learned that Grace had expanded her activities to include a Sunday morning service, he told her he would stay the weekend to attend. Sunday morning, Ray Faus had a front row seat in Grace's congregation. After the service he waited for a word with her.

"I'm going to keep looking around for a couple of days more," he told her. "If I find something, I'll let you know. If not, I'll call to say goodbye before I leave."

"Well now, let's turn it over to the One Power, Ray. Know that, as children of God, our good is open and flowing to all of us, all of the time. Know that Omnipresence, Truth, includes your right employment at the right remuneration. We trust God and thank God that this is so, for so it is."

Two days later Ray Faus recalled those words with awe. After another day's fruitless search, he had sat down on a park bench to rest. He wasn't going to waste any more time, he told himself. This evening he would pack his bag and in the morning he would leave for Denver. His plans set, Ray reached into his pocket for the little copy of *The Impersonal Life*, which he carried with him throughout his travels, and began to read. Its familiar phrases greeted him like old friends and bolstered him now.

Ray stood up after awhile and returned the book to his pocket. Then as if being led by the hand he walked across the street to the Commerce Building. Entering, he went down the hall, walked into one of the offices and to the desk. There was no one behind it. He looked about for a moment, then sat down. Within five minutes a pleasant-faced woman entered at the back from an adjoining office. She looked at Ray and said,

"What are your qualifications, sir?"

"I'm a stocks and bonds salesman," he said, going to stand at the desk, and stated his background and work experience. As he spoke, the woman wrote the information on a tablet.

"Please wait here," she said. "Just have a chair. I'll be back shortly."

After twenty minutes the woman reappeared. She smiled and said,

"We have a position for you, Mr. Faus. Your background and experience qualify you perfectly for a position with *The*

National Recovery Administration. One of our clerks is preparing the contract. It will be ready in ten minutes."

Inquiring about the salary, Ray was speechless at the figure the woman quoted. He nodded in agreement and went back to his chair.

That evening he related his success to the director of the YMCA. The gray-haired administrator looked at Ray skeptically.

"You mean you applied for a job with the government *today* and you've been *hired already*? That's—*impossible,* son! Are you sure you heard correctly? It takes *months* for a job like that to come through! You've got to go through all kinds of red tape—interviews, reference checks, conferences, et cetera!"

"Sir, all I can tell you is that before I left the Commerce Department today, I signed on the dotted line! I'm to report to work at eight o'clock Monday morning. And now if you'll excuse me, I've got to call a very special lady."

He walked across the lobby and telephoned Grace.

CHAPTER XV

ORDINATION

Nothing was so thrilling to Grace as watching her people grow into the realization of the All Good which is God and their Divine Heritage of All Good as children of God. With *Basic Principles of Truth* and *Spiritual Psychology* completed, her students were ready now for their third course in Divine Science study: *Introduction to the Bible*, the metaphysical interpretation of the Bible. To do justice to the subject, Grace invited the Reverend Ada B. Fay of New York to come to Washington to teach the year-long course. Hospitality arrangements were made by Mathilde Rochon, who again came forth with her overwhelming generosity. The New York minister-teacher would live at the Rochon home as Mathilde's and Grace's guest.

During her third month with Grace and her people, the Reverend Fay made a startling recommendation. Sitting with Grace and Mathilde at dinner one evening, she said, "Grace, you should be ordained."

"Why, what do you mean?"

"I mean you should be ordained as a Divine Science minister."

"*What? Me? A minister?*" Grace looked incredulous.

"Yes, you. A minister."

Grace put both her hands on the table and laughed. Then noting Mrs. Fay's seriousness, she said, "But why? I'm — a teacher. My classes and my Sunday services are going quite well as things are, don't you think so?"

"Yes, of course I do. But you could be of much more service to your people if you were an ordained minister—you could perform the marriage ceremony, and conduct christenings and funerals. These needs of your people must be met, you know. They will become part of your responsibilities as leader of the Divine Science work in Washington. You should prepare yourself through ordination to meet them, my dear. I intend to so advise the mother church in Denver."

Through the Reverend Fay's recommendation, Grace was ordained minister of the Washington Divine Science Church in 1934 by Dr. Harvey Hardman, minister of the Divine Science Church and College of Denver. In a brief ceremony Dr. Hardman presented Grace to her congregation, which now numbered fifty.

Inspired by Grace's ordination, the members of the congregation began talking of incorporating their church, complete with a board of trustees and membership. Persuading their minister of the advantages of such action, they drew up plans and held meetings for the election of officers. The incorporation was completed later that year and marked the group's second major step forward in 1934.

They decided to celebrate. All fifty members of the First Divine Science Church and College of Washington, D.C. met at the *Green Parrot Restaurant* for an evening of dinner and fellowship. Citing May 4, 1934, as their church's official date of incorporation, Jimmy Bost, the group's master of ceremonies, proposed a toast:

"To the Reverend Grace Patch, sent to our city to share the Light of Truth with all of us, and to faithfully teach Truth to all who seek, to all who are interested, to all who would walk by Truth's Light."

In response, Grace cited Omnipresence with them as they

moved forward together in the Light into a greater awareness of Truth.

From that hour, the members of that pioneer group were united in One Spirit and One Purpose, and were to function together with their minister-teacher as One Mind for twelve fruitful years.

At the close of each Sunday morning service Grace walked down the center aisle and stood by the door to meet and greet her parishioners individually. One Sunday in April, 1936, Grace noticed a woman standing at the side of the room whom she had never seen before. Beautiful, and fashionably-dressed, the newcomer waited for a private word with the minister. When the last parishioner had gone the woman walked toward Grace and said, "Good morning, Mrs. Patch. I'm Mrs. Edna Lister, minister of the Society of the Healing Christ in Seattle, Washington." Smiling, she extended her hand to Grace.

"How do you do, Mrs. Lister. How wonderful to have you with us this morning. Will you be in Washington long?"

"Just until four o'clock today. Then I'm taking the train to New York. I came to invite you to the International New Thought Alliance Congress which will meet in July at the Waldorf Astoria in New York."

"Thank you, Mrs. Lister. Thank you very much."

"You *must* attend, Mrs. Patch. I'm putting your name on the list of platform speakers. I'll be counting on you to be right up there with the others."

"Oh, — I can't attend the Congress, Mrs. Lister. I'm sorry. It would be impossible for me to go to New York in July."

"But why, Mrs. Patch? We're counting on you. We want to have the Washington Divine Science work represented at the Congress by its minister."

"Well, there are several reasons, Mrs. Lister. I—just couldn't manage it."

"Let's have dinner and we'll talk about it. Are you free for an hour or so?"

"Yes."

At dinner in the Mayflower Hotel's *Presidential Room*, Edna Lister said briskly, "Now then, Grace. About the International New Thought Alliance Congress coming up in July. You've got plenty of time to get ready—plenty of time to prepare your talk. On what subject would you like to speak?"

Grace laughed. "Wait just a minute, Mrs. Lister—"

"Please call me Edna."

"Edna—look here. I don't have the money for anything like that. I certainly don't have the clothes for anything like that, either. I can't go."

"Yes you *can*. And you *will*. And you'll have plenty of money and plenty of clothes, too. Let's remember our Basis: Omnipresence. All Good with us! Abundance, Supply, with us! '*The silver is mine, the gold is mine, the cattle on a thousand hills are mine. Son, thou are ever with Me, and all that I have is thine.*' You know those words well, Grace. They were spoken for you, too."

A few Sundays later, the president of the Board of Trustees of the Washington Divine Science Church announced to the congregation that their minister had been invited to speak at the International New Thought Alliance Congress in New York in July. At the close of the service that morning, Mathilde Rochon approached the Board's president as he stood talking with Grace. She too would attend the INTA Congress, Mathilde told him. It had been years since she'd taken a vacation from her job in her parents' beauty salon. As a gift to her minister-teacher, she would pay for the room that the two of them would share.

When Grace visited her mother to make arrangements for Diana's care during her absence in July, the elder Grace said to the younger,

"Gracie, I still think this religion you're mixed up in is nothing but a lot of foolishness! But, if you're going to speak at the Waldorf Astoria in New York, you've got to *look the part*! Come over tomorrow morning and we'll go downtown to choose patterns and fabrics. I'll get to work right away. You'll have a good-looking wardrobe for your July convention. *My* treat — it's on *me*."

One month later Grace was on stage in the ballroom of the Waldorf Astoria Hotel with the featured speakers of the International New Thought Alliance Congress, seated beside the renowned Emmet Fox, minister of The Church of the Healing Christ in New York City. Able to hear Dr. Fox's modulated tones as he talked with the person on his left, Grace tried to concentrate on the INTA Principles printed on the folder she held in her hand:

"We affirm the freedom of each soul as to choice and as to belief, and would not, by the adoption of any declaration of principles, limit such freedom. The essence of the New Thought is Truth, and each individual must be loyal to the Truth he sees. The windows of his soul must be kept open at each moment for the higher light, and his mind must be always hospitable to each new inspiration.

"We affirm the Good. This is supreme, universal and everlasting. Man is made in the image of the Good, and evil and pain are but the tests and correctives that appear when his thought does not reflect the full glory of this image.

"We affirm health, which is every man's divine inheritance. Man's body is his holy temple. Every function of it, every cell of it, is intelligent, and is shaped, ruled, repaired, and controlled by mind. He whose body is full of light is full of health.

"We affirm the divine supply. He who serves God and man in the full understanding of the law of compensation shall not lack. Within us are unused resources of energy and power. He who lives with his whole being, and thus expresses fullness, shall reap fullness in return.

"We affirm the teaching of Christ that the Kingdom of Heaven is within us, that we are one with the Father, that we should not judge, that we should love one another, that we should heal the sick, that we should return good for evil, that we should minister to others.

"We of the International New Thought Alliance affirm the new thought of God as Universal Love, Life, Truth and Joy, in whom we live, move, and have our being, and by whom we are held together; that His mind is our mind now, that realizing our oneness with Him means love, truth, peace, health, and plenty, not only in our own lives but in the giving out of these fruits of the Spirit to others.

"We affirm these things, not as a profession, but practice; not on one day of the week, but in every hour and minute of every day, sleeping and waking; not in the ministry of a few, but in a service that includes the democracy of all; not in words alone, but in the innermost thoughts of the heart expressed in living the life. 'By their fruits ye shall know them.'

"We affirm Heaven here and now, the life everlasting that becomes conscious immortality, the communion of mind with mind throughout the universe of thoughts, the nothingness of all error and negation, including death, the variety in unity that produces the individual expressions of the One-Life, and the quickened realization of the indwelling God in each soul that is making a new heaven and a new earth.

"We affirm that the universe is spiritual and we are spiritual beings. This is the Christ message to the twentieth century, and it is a message not so much of words as of works. We now have the golden opportunity to form a real Christ movement. Let us build our house upon this rock, and nothing can prevail against it. This is the vision and mission of the Alliance."

At that moment Emmet Fox turned to speak to Grace. Suddenly she was face to face with the famous minister-author whose books about Truth were receiving worldwide acclaim.

"How do you do, Dr. Fox," Grace responded when he introduced himself to her. "I'm Grace Patch of The First Divine Science Church, Washington, D.C."

Emmet Fox expressed his interest in the beginnings and growth of Divine Science in Washington. Learning that Grace had been a student of Nona Brooks, Dr. Fox told her of his close friendship with the Denver Divine Science leader. It was Nona Brooks who had ordained him into the Divine Science ministry.

Ten minutes remained until the Congress would begin. As Grace and her fascinating platform partner continued their exchange, she discovered that Emmet Fox had been born in Ireland of Catholic parents, educated in England, had attended a Jesuit college before coming into New Thought, and had been strongly influenced by his good friend, Judge Thomas Troward. He had never married. His mother and sister lived in England and he returned periodically to visit them. As a matter of fact, he was sailing that night for England. Immediately after his address to the Congress, he would leave for a six-week visit abroad with his family.

Then the auditorium quieted. President Edna Lister walked to the podium. She welcomed the New Thought representatives from churches and centers throughout the world and introduced the International New Thought Alliance officers. Then with a special ring to her words, Mrs. Lister presented the first speaker of the evening. Rising to a burst of vigorously sustained applause, the inimitable Emmet Fox strode to the podium.

The total Congress experience represented new dimensions in Truth teaching for Grace.

"It's good to be home again," she told her congregation the next Sunday morning. "Mathilde Rochon traveled with me to New York, but I had every one of you there with me in my heart. I bring you greetings from Dr. Emmet Fox, minister of the Church of the Healing Christ in New York City, whose books are such an inspiration to all of us."

She shared with her eager listeners the substance of her conversation with Dr. Fox.

"The next morning, while having breakfast at a little shop, I looked up to see a white-haired gentleman sitting alone at a nearby table. 'Why, that's Henry Victor Morgan!' I thought. I went to him and told him that I certainly knew who he was! We became friends immediately and had a wonderful talk. Henry Victor Morgan is the poet laureate of the INTA and minister of the Church of the Healing Christ in Tacoma, Washington. He's in his seventies now—a striking-looking man with beautiful white hair. He has a bright red car that he whizzes around in! He too sends greetings to you.

"I met Ada Coxe Fisher, one of our outstanding New Thought teachers, and Elizabeth Towne, a great big beautiful woman full of life and joy and harmony and beauty! Elizabeth Towne is the editor and publisher of *The Nautilus*, one of the first New Thought periodicals to appear in the United States and a wonderful guide to the understanding of Truth to millions of people everywhere.

"The brilliant young Raymond Charles Barker, minister of the Unity Church in Rochester, New York, invited me to a gathering at his home where I met his parents and sister. Dr. Barker is a handsome, talented young man whose enthusiasm, energy, and dynamic ideas contributed importantly to the Congress.

"In all, it was a glorious time of fellowship with members of New Thought churches, centers, and societies from all over the world—an uplifting, expanding experience for which I am very grateful."

In his usual place in the congregation, the last row near the window, Ray Faus listened interestedly. Ray had joined the church soon after he began working in Washington and attended services regularly. After the service he was last in line to greet Grace.

"Grace, you were very inspiring today. I'd like to take the classwork. May I?"

"Of course you may! It will be wonderful to have you with us."

"Are there any prerequisites?"

"Only one—interest in the Truth. That's the only prerequisite."

"I am interested."

"Then join us. You are most welcome."

"Thank you, Grace. And may I ask permission to take the minister and her charming daughter to dinner now that church is over?"

"That would be lovely. Yes, thank you, Ray."

Then turning to Diana, Grace said, "Diana, Mr. Faus has invited us to have dinner with him."

Diana had met Ray Faus soon after he came to Washington. The two of them were friends. Diana took the hand Ray held out to her. "Thank you," she said.

Grace put her books and materials in the box marked "Storage." She locked the studio then and the three of them left to share the first of many Sunday afternoons together.

In mid-August the Penwomen moved from Stoneleigh Court to larger quarters in the Grafton Hotel at Connecticut Avenue and LaSalle Street, and moved The Divine Science Church and College along with them.

Some very distinguished Washingtonians came to church services at the Grafton, located across from the Mayflower Hotel. Grace felt no concern now about the presence of dignitaries at her services. She welcomed their interest and was thrilled by it.

At the Grafton, Grace met Mrs. Margaret Cresson, daughter of Daniel Chester French, the renowned sculptor who created *The Seated Lincoln* for the Lincoln Memorial. Mrs. Cresson was herself a sculptress, Grace learned. But for several years now she had been unable to pursue her art. After her father passed away in 1931, her mother became very ill. Since then, Margaret's time was devoted to caring for her.

"I have heard that Divine Science offers spiritual healing," Mrs. Cresson said to Grace. "That's why I came. I would like help for my invalid mother."

Margaret Cresson came to Grace regularly for spiritual treatment and guidance. Her mother began to improve. In a relatively short time she recovered completely, and Margaret was free to return to her art. Thrilled by the change in her circumstances, Mrs. Cresson joined the church and shared a close, lifelong friendship with the minister. Throughout the years Grace was a frequent guest at Margaret's home in Stockbridge, Massachusetts, the house that contained the studio in which her father had executed his famous works.

Mrs. Anna Rogers Minor, Regent General of the Society of the Daughters of the American Revolution, introduced herself to Grace after church one Sunday.

"I came because I saw your ad, and noted that the minister was a woman. I'm very much interested in the progress being made by women in the various professions. I congratulate you on your initiative and success in undertaking the ministry of this church."

Then came the most revered and most beloved of all. Dr. Nona L. Brooks arrived in Washington and immediately went to Grace at the Grafton. In a thrilling address to the First Divine Science Church congregation, Dr. Brooks expressed her great joy and satisfaction in the establishment and growth of Divine Science in the nation's capital. She gave her blessings to the church, the congregation, and to the minister, who had been her student.

Meeting privately with Grace later that week, Dr. Brooks authorized her to train and ordain other qualified persons for the ministry.

Astonished, Grace expressed her reluctance. "Oh—but Dr. Brooks—*that is an awesome responsibility.*"

"I assure you that you are eminently qualified, my dear. It is, therefore, your responsibility."

It was not until May, 1938, that the full import of Nona Brooks' conferral registered with Grace. It was the last Sunday of the month and a great day for the minister, Board of Trustees, and the twelve students who comprised the first graduating class of the Divine Science Church and College of Washington, D.C.

In a brief ceremony at the end of the service, Grace commended her twelve students for the earnestness and application with which they had approached the four-year Divine Science course of study. She emphasized that the true measure of their mastery lay in the minute-by-minute, hour-by-hour living of the Truth that had been revealed to them. At the close of the exercises, impressive in their simplicity and spiritual import, each student received a certificate of graduation.

Alone in her room that night, Grace put aside the book she had been reading to look back on the activities of her day. In her mind she pictured the faces of her students as they had sat before her that morning: Mathilde Rochon, whose generosity had been so helpful to the establishment of the work; William Humphries; Wilbur Simonson; Sylvia Wentworth; Horace and Gordana Ashton, the dynamic couple whose enthusiasm and vitality added so much to the group; Carolyn Millichamp; Grace Williams; Ray Faus; Florence Frisbie; Thelma Harper; and Addie Rae Peoples, a teacher's delight. Addie was brilliant, conscientious, dedicated. From the beginning, Addie's steadily-unfolding consciousness had been gratifying to observe. By her fourth year of training, Addie understood her relationship to the Divine and had taken on the discipline of living the Truth.

Suddenly Grace remembered the last conversation she'd had with Nona Brooks. During their talk, Dr. Brooks had said: *"I assure you that you are eminently qualified to train and ordain other persons well-suited for the ministry. It is, therefore, your responsibility. You will be led, my dear. All ordination is of God. Remember, it is the Father that doeth the works."*

In that moment Grace knew that Addie Rae Peoples would advance to the higher work and become first a practitioner, then a Divine Science minister.

At six o'clock the next morning, Grace answered the telephone and learned that her mother had been admitted to the hospital. At the hospital Grace was told that her mother's diabetic condition had caused an acute infection of the left leg.

"Now, Gracie, don't be thinking of using your Divine Science on me! If I'm ill, I'm *ill*. And that's *that*," Grace Lightfoot told her daughter, attempting a smile as she lay in her bed.

"All right, Mama. I wouldn't unless you asked me to," the younger Grace assured her.

Grace Lightfoot's condition worsened. After three weeks the doctors stated that immediate amputation of the leg was necessary.

It was then that Grace stepped in.

"We will wait a few days," she told the attending physician.

"It will be too late then. It must be done now," he replied.

Grace was insistent. "We want to wait a few days. It is my mother's wish also."

Three days later the doctor on duty reported an improvement in Grace Lightfoot's condition. The infection showed signs of clearing. The amputation would not need to be performed. It was no less than a miracle, he added—one of those rare occurrences that defied explanation and baffled the medical profession.

After the doctor had gone from the room, Grace Lightfoot looked up at her daughter, her eyes brimming with tears.

"I think you've got something there, after all, Gracie," she conceded, reaching for her daughter's hand. "Yes, I really believe you *do*."

Two weeks later Grace Lightfoot sat in the congregation of the First Divine Science Church and heard The Reverend Grace Patch for the first time. A few Sundays later she came again, and had dinner afterward with Grace, Diana, Ray Faus, and Ray's son, Jim.

"So you're beginning to like Divine Science, Mrs. Lightfoot?" Ray teased her as they drove along.

"Nonsense. I only go to that church to see what Gracie is *wearing*. Since I make all of her clothes, I like to see her in them. And if I do say so myself, Gracie, that mauve is stunning on you."

But before Grace Lightfoot made her transition in 1940, she had come to accept Divine Science and its Principle of Truth.

CHAPTER XVI

TOGETHER A FAMILY

A deep, companionable bond formed between Grace and
Ray Faus. They went out evenings occasionally, and spent
their Sunday afternoons together. The tall, good-looking Ray
had a genial personality and a delightful sense of humor. He
and Grace were interested in the same things, and enjoyed
each other's company. An earnest, dedicated student of
Divine Science now, Ray had read practically all of the books
in the church library and liked talking with Grace about
them. He understood Grace's work, and respected and admired her dedication to the Divine Science ministry. Ray Faus
never considered Grace's profession an unusual one for a
woman. It was only natural for a woman to be involved in
helping people and comforting people, he believed; it was
only natural for a woman to be involved in teaching and
counseling. A woman in the ministry, Ray felt, was functioning in as characteristic a role as a nurse, school-teacher, or
secretary.

Within a year Ray asked Grace to marry him. Startled,
Grace replied with a tactful negative. She thought at once of
her deep commitment to her responsibilities as Divine Science
minister and teacher. With her move to Washington, these
had woven themselves into the entire fabric of her life. It
seemed, Grace felt, as if she were married to her church. Ray
said nothing more. When he asked her again three months
later, the answer was *yes*.

The next year Grace became Mrs. Ray Faus. The two families made a compatible unit — Grace, the teen-age Diana, Ray, and Jim, Ray's young son. They moved into a modest home on Sixteenth Street and lived together comfortably and happily.

Their move was paralleled by the Penwomen's move to larger quarters in the Burlington Hotel. And again the Penwomen took the First Divine Science Church of Washington right along with them. The Penwomen's need for larger facilities coincided with the church's need for greater seating capacity. The spacious room at the Burlington provided this along with excellent acoustics.

On this, the church's second Sunday in its new setting, Grace sat in the speaker's chair near the podium listening to the soloist, Kathryn Slagle. As Kathryn's beautiful soprano voice filled the room Grace marvelled at the way all their needs had been met. The talented Miss Slagle herself had come to them in a unique way. Grace first heard of her at The International New Thought Alliance Congress in New York. Someone had come to her and said,

"I understand that you're from Washington, D.C. There's a very fine singer there, you know — Miss Kathryn Slagle — a truly magnificent voice —"

When she returned Grace telephoned Kathryn Slagle and asked her to sing at her services. Kathryn sang for them the following Sunday. A beautiful young woman with an exquisite voice, Kathryn inspired the entire congregation. She had been with them each Sunday since. Developing a deep interest in Truth, she enrolled in the classes and became Grace's devoted student.

Noticing a movement at the back of the church Grace looked up to see a well-dressed, distinguished-looking gentleman being seated by the usher.

"I've seen him before," she thought. *"He looks like — a minister!"*

After the service, Grace walked down the center aisle to her place by the door. Greeting her parishioners, she came face to face with the stranger. As she extended her hand to him he smiled and said,

"Good morning, Grace. I'm Harry Gaze."

Harry Gaze! Of course! She had met him nearly twenty years ago in Denver—heard him speak at the church when he lectured there as Dr. Brooks' guest. Grace's eyes shone with pleasure. How thrilling to see him again—to have him here in her very own church—listening to *her* sermon!

Later that year, Grace and her congregation were visited by another outstanding Divine Science leader. Dr. Harvey Hardman of the Denver church came to Washington to conduct a special Sunday morning service. He lauded the growth of the church and gave his blessings to the work, the minister, and the congregation.

Thrilled that their 'growing was showing,' the membership wanted to establish a location of their own. To this end they set up a building fund, which, just a few years later in 1945, totalled over ten thousand dollars.

The group took special pride in the church library. All of them worked together to maintain this facility which had evolved from Grace's personal collection of books and periodicals. Through contributions made by members and friends, it had grown substantially. The library was staffed by volunteers and its stock was available to the congregation for borrowing or purchase each Sunday after the service.

The Divine Science Church body was a remarkably adaptable group. When the Penwomen decided later to buy a home, the Church membership voted to go out on their own. They rented space in *The Pink Palace* at 2601 Sixteenth Street, owned by the Eastern Star.

"This is not a building—this is *heaven!*" Grace remarked to the Board of Trustees after a week in their new location. "Carrying out the work in this beautiful place is pure joy!"

The magnificent structure, once the home of the Marshall Fields of Chicago, had been elegantly designed for entertaining on a grand scale. The ballroom served now as The Divine Science Church auditorium. The church's rented suite included an office for Grace and classrooms.

They continued at this location for a long time. Then a letter came from the secretary of the Eastern Star advising Grace and the Board of Trustees that the building had been sold. Pushed out of their nest, minister, Board, and membership set out to find new quarters. They chose the American Legion Building on Fifteenth Street.

But soon there were complaints from the elderly and the handicapped. Classes were held in a room on the third floor, and there were stairs to climb. They objected, openly voicing their dissatisfaction. Through notes and telephone calls, they aired their grievances to Grace and chided her for her inconsiderate choice of location. There was no elevator, they pointed out. Unless an elevator were made available, they would be unable to attend.

At a special meeting, the group voted to change its location. This time they rented space in the Raleigh Hotel. At the Raleigh theirs was an attractive room with a large seating capacity. The management allotted them space near the lobby each Sunday morning for a table on which books and periodicals could be displayed.

The easily accessible Raleigh location pleased everyone. Yet for Grace and the volunteers who helped her, transporting the trunkful of books to and from the Raleigh each Sunday was a heavy, strenuous task about which they said nothing. Arriving early each Sunday morning, they arranged the books and periodicals on the table to accommodate the congregation before and after the service. Afterward, they tallied the loan and sales chart, repacked the books, and returned the trunk to their storeroom at the American Legion.

At the Raleigh there was a marked increase in church attendance and book circulation reached a new high. For many newcomers, Truth as presented by Divine Science was an oasis in the desert of fallible religious dogma, just as it had been for the dedicated members who worked together now to make Truth available to all.

Throughout her ministry Grace found Washington a transient city, and often her mail contained letters and cards from former students and members of her congregation who had gone to other cities and countries. Although she missed these staunch friends in her immediate environment, Grace took the larger view of their absence, knowing that wherever they went they carried the consciousness of Truth with them, serving as a kind of leaven as they traveled throughout the world.

Going through her mail one Saturday morning, Grace came upon a manila envelope postmarked *New York*. It contained a thin volume with the fascinating title, "The Man Who Tapped the Secrets of the Universe." With it was a note from Margaret Tyler, a close friend and former student.

"This man Walter Russell is phenomenal—a modern-day Leonardo da Vinci," Margaret wrote. "Dr. Russell is a scientist, artist, musician, inventor, writer, philosopher, and teacher of Universal Principle here in New York's Carnegie Hall. I just *had* to send this book to you. Its message parallels your teaching to a 'T'."

In less than a week, Margaret telephoned Grace from New York.

"Have you read the book I sent you?" she asked enthusiastically.

"As a matter of fact, Margaret, I haven't. It's been a busy week. I'm waiting for a break so that I really can get into it."

"Well, you had better read it soon because I've already made an appointment with Walter Russell so that the two of you can meet. I'm driving to Washington Sunday, and I'm going to bring you back to New York with me for a few days."

"You are!" Grace laughed.

"Yes, I am! So make arrangements to be away for part of the coming week. I'm taking you to Dr. Russell's studio Tuesday. We're due there at ten o'clock in the morning."

Before Margaret Tyler arrived in Washington the following Sunday, Grace read and re-read Glenn Clark's *The Man Who Tapped the Secrets of the Universe*. With the first chapter she began looking forward to meeting Dr. Walter Russell with a thrill of excitement she had not felt since her early days in Washington when she attended a special conference at the Washington Academy of Science and met and heard Dr. Albert Einstein, Dr. Robert A. Millikan, Sir James Jeans, and Sir Arthur Eddington.

At Carnegie Hall in New York the following Tuesday, Grace entered the studio of Walter Russell with her friend and found herself surrounded by magnificent statuary, exquisite paintings, and all manner of resplendent art. In that unique setting she was introduced by Margaret Tyler to Dr. Walter Russell.

For Grace, the book she had read only days ago about this humble man of multi-faceted genius was suddenly translated into living form as she looked into the brilliant, kindly eyes and clasped the welcoming hand of the artist known as the man who tapped the secrets of the universe.

He invited his guests to sit by the fireplace, and laid a fresh fire. He took a chair beside the two women then and began talking. The conversation, rich, fascinating, embraced a variety of subjects. He was silent then, thoughtful as he watched the rise and fall of the flames, and the three of them sat quietly enjoying the companionable experience.

At length Dr. Russell rose to place another log on the fire, and after further conversation with his guests, went to his desk and took some keys from a drawer. Walking across the studio to a small room at the back, he took some papers from a locked metal cabinet and returned with them to his chair.

"I keep these writings under lock and key because no one seems to understand them. They contain the substance of that which came to me many years ago during a period of Cosmic Instruction. At that time I sat writing day and night, entering by hand all that was being revealed to me. One in my family thought I had gone mad and telephoned our lawyer. But when he examined the papers, the lawyer assured her that the writings were not the expression of an insane man, but, rather, valuable records of unprecedented scientific and philosophical concepts.

"I believe you will appreciate the substance of these writings, Grace. If you will permit me, I will read portions of them to you."

Dr. Russell began then. Grace sat fascinated as she heard the articulations of the Absolute uttered in the rich, resonant tones of this unassuming man to whom the Universe had voiced its secrets.

When he had finished, Grace said quietly, "Yes, Dr. Russell, I understand what you have read, what you have so graciously shared here this morning. I am most grateful to you—and to Mrs. Tyler—for the privilege of this experience. Thank you. Dr. Russell, I wonder if I might ask—would you consider coming to Washington at some future time to speak to my congregation—to present some of your concepts and experiences? It would mean so much to all of us. Your visit to our city would be a great influence for good."

Walter Russell accepted Grace's invitation, eventually arriving in Washington, D.C. to address her congregation and to remain to offer a course in metaphysics at the Washington Hotel.

Shortly after his visit to the nation's capital, he began a tour of the United States, painting and lecturing as he went from place to place.

Later, when Walter Russell and his beautiful young bride Lao chose Swannanoa, Virginia, as their mountain-top home, Grace and Ray Faus stayed with them the summer of that year to help the couple settle into their gorgeous marble palace residence and to enroll as students in the first class taught by Dr. Russell in his inspiring new surroundings.

CHAPTER XVII

A GRAVE CONCERN

The New Deal, President Roosevelt's plan of action to restore the economy of the depression-ridden nation, had begun to take shape shortly after his inauguration in 1933. Immediate passage of emergency bank bills put an end to the banking crisis. People stopped hoarding money. Prices of securities and goods started to climb. The American people began to realize a sense of security and unity as the economy steadily rose during Roosevelt's first and second terms.

Then in 1941 America entered World War II. To equip and supply the American armed forces and their Allies, defense-minded citizens united as never before. Working shoulder-to-shoulder they manned round-the-clock shifts to achieve production goals unapproximated in the past.

Now, in 1944, business and industry flourished. The National Recovery Administration, for which Ray Faus had worked so long, became an obsolete agency. When it closed Ray immediately looked around for another job. But the prospects left him dissatisfied. Discouraged, Ray suddenly began drinking again. Shocked at the discovery, Grace experienced piercing disappointment.

Her personal and professional life were challengingly complex now. Two weeks ago, the management of the Raleigh Hotel had sent a letter to the Divine Science Church advising that their rent would be doubled upon receipt of notice.

Taken aback, the Board of Trustees and membership protested. It was more than they could afford, they informed the Raleigh management. In a specially called meeting they studied alternatives, then voted to go back to the moderately-priced American Legion Building. In less than a week the move was completed.

Again the First Divine Science Church was functioning on Fifteenth Street in the American Legion Building. And again Grace was deluged with complaints from the elderly and the handicapped. Grace submitted their grievances to the Board of Trustees. The Board studied them and maintained that there was nothing to be done about them. The American Legion rent was reasonable. It was the most they were willing to pay.

At the next month's meeting of the Board of Trustees, it was voted that the Reverend Addie Rae Peoples be placed in charge of the church work while Grace vacationed during July and August. Ordained by Grace earlier that year, Addie was delighted at the prospect of carrying on the summer work. She welcomed the opportunity and looked forward to the invaluable experience it would provide for her.

Grace's vacation was weighted with care concerning her husband's alcoholism. Ray was drinking heavily now. This prevented his holding a job for long and he went from one place of employment to another. To supplement her income from the church, Grace worked summers for the *National Symphony Orchestra* directing seating section sales. Diana was a student at Mary Washington College now and the extra money was needed.

In Florida with friends for the summer, Diana had a job and was taking flying lessons. She was having a wonderful time, she wrote her family. She and her flying instructor had become good friends.

After a flight review with her instructor one day, Diana confided her concern about her stepfather's drinking.

"Get the book *Alcoholics Anonymous* and have him read it. Thousands have been cured by its methods since it came out in '39," her teacher advised her.

Diana bought the book. She knew that her stepfather was an avid reader and that one of the techniques he used for sobering was the reading of deep, heavy books. He kept a group of these on his night table. When Diana returned home in August, she placed *Alcoholics Anonymous* among them. Ray read it.

The book led Ray to inquire about *Alcoholics Anonymous* in Washington. He learned that there was an *AA* group within walking distance of his home. Ray began attending *AA* meetings, and Grace was pleased that he had somewhere to go that interested him. He had stayed home for months. Ray did all his drinking at home. For that, Grace was grateful. It made it easier for her to hide his condition. As a minister, she felt compelled to keep it hidden. She told no one.

With the approach of summer's end the Board of Trustees called a meeting to discuss the church's fall and winter schedule. The Reverend Addie Rae Peoples' handling of the summer work was reviewed. Her leadership would terminate when Grace returned to the pulpit the first Sunday in September. The meeting was thrown open then for ideas and suggestions. There were several.

Some of them felt that the Board should have the jurisdiction to decide which classes the minister should conduct, and when and where they should be conducted. Also, they believed it essential that the Board should review and approve all class curriculum content prior to presentation. The suggestions were made a motion, and the Board voted in favor. The treasurer was then called upon to make her report.

Building Fund contributions were coming in steadily, Carrie Morgan reported to the Board. Contributions were generous and averaged one hundred dollars per week. The Fund figure now totalled over ten thousand dollars.

Mrs. Morgan interrupted her report to say that she always dreaded taking the money home with her—dreaded carrying it with her at work on Mondays until she could get to the bank later in the day. She feared being robbed. Would someone who was free Monday mornings be willing to take the responsibility? No one was available. All of them had early morning work schedules. Grace volunteered then and she was put in charge of depositing Building Fund contributions and the plate collection at the bank each Monday morning. Grateful, Carrie Morgan expressed her relief to Grace and the members of the Board.

The meeting adjourned and Grace returned home to wait for Ray, who was attending a meeting of the *AA*. Motivated by the book Diana had given him, Ray had gone on to become a member of *Alcoholics Anonymous*.

Months later, coming in from the January meeting, he said to his wife enthusiastically, "Grace, I want you to go with me to the next *AA* meeting!"

Grace looked up from her reading. "Ray, *how* could you ask a thing like that of me? I've had *enough* of drunkards! A roomful would be more than I could take. *No*, Ray."

She regretted the words instantly. She had not meant to hurt him.

"It's all right, Grace. I—understand how you feel. I've put you through a lot, I know."

On a Thursday evening three weeks later Grace put on a dress Ray especially liked and went with him as his guest to the February meeting of *Alcoholics Anonymous*.

Entering the *AA* clubroom with her husband, Grace looked about in amazement. Surely these attractive, distinguished-looking, well-dressed, dignified people weren't *alcoholics*! She moved about the room with Ray as he introduced her to the members and their families. Here were people of all occupations and professions.

The meeting was called to order promptly. There followed a reading and review of the *AA*'s *Twelve Steps*. After hearing them, Grace turned to Ray and said softly,

"Where in the world did they get them? They're straight *Divine Science*!"

"That's right," Ray answered. "They're taken from Emmet Fox's *Sermon on the Mount*."

When the meeting was over, Grace found herself being greeted by fine-looking, intelligent, well-informed men and women with whom conversation was a delight. Passing a corner table as she and Ray made their way to the door, Grace was surprised and amused when a lanky gentleman sprang from his chair, patted her on the shoulder, and said encouragingly,

"You just stay with it, Girlie! You'll make it! Just stay with it!"

Ray continued to attend the *AA* meetings regularly. Coming home from the April meeting, he handed his wife a small white envelope and said,

"Grace, I was asked to deliver this to you."

The envelope contained a note to Grace inviting her to be the guest speaker at the *Alcoholics Anonymous* Annual Family Dinner. Ray shrugged his shoulders.

"They really liked you, Grace. They know you're a minister, and would like to have you address them. I personally had nothing to do with it. Please don't feel you have to accept."

"But I *want to*, Ray," she told him. "I would like very much to address them. I consider the invitation an honor."

Grace's appearance as guest speaker at the *Alcoholics*

Anonymous Annual Family Dinner in May paved the way to new and wider opportunities for service to people who were among the most wonderful she had ever known. In speaking to them, Grace expressed her gratitude for the privilege of meeting and getting to know the men and women of *AA* and their families. She voiced her understanding of the problems faced by the alcoholic—and by the wives, husbands, children, and parents of the alcoholic. She told of the anxiety and stress that being married to an alcoholic caused in her own life and of living in dread of social and professional repercussions.

Truth, Grace told her audience, was the Source from which she derived her strength to cope, and emphasized that this same Source, when turned to, would supply each of them with the strength and power to triumph over their individual problems. This Truth that was in them and with them would supply their every need.

"I would have each of you remember with me," Grace said in conclusion, "that being in Truth doesn't mean we will never have problems to meet. It does mean that, if and when problems come, we will know how to meet them."

They gave her a standing ovation.

In the weeks that followed, Grace was thrilled to see several *AA* members at her Sunday services. *AA* wives, husbands, sons, daughters, and parents began coming to her office during the week for counselling and guidance. Grace welcomed them warmly. She felt deep love and respect for all of them. These were among the most courageous people she had ever known.

After the service one Sunday, a woman standing in line to greet Grace took her hand and said in a hushed voice,

"Reverend Faus, would you be willing to speak to my daughter? She needs help."

"Certainly. Have her come see me."

"But she's—*she's an awful drunk!*"

"That's *O.K.* I will be glad to see her. Have her come."

The next day the young woman entered Grace's office and spent the entire afternoon talking earnestly about her problem and listening to the serene minister whose gentle words filled her with peace.

Grace never saw the young woman again. But years later the girl's mother returned to tell her that a miracle had taken place on that long-ago afternoon. Since the time of her visit with Grace that day, her daughter had never taken another drink.

CHAPTER XVIII

BEGINNING ANEW

During the summer of 1945 the Reverend Addie Rae Peoples again filled the pulpit of the First Divine Science Church while the Reverend Grace Faus vacationed until September.

Now, the afternoon of August tenth, Grace walked along Sixteenth Street quickly, eager to get home and out of the heat after her day of work at the *National Symphony*.

The summer had followed a memory-evoking spring. In March, her beloved teacher and mentor, Dr. Nona L. Brooks, died in Denver eight days before her eighty-fourth birthday. One month later on April 12, a shocked world received the news of President Franklin Roosevelt's death.

As she walked along, Grace acknowledged a settling influence in her life now. Ray was making good progress in the *AA* program and she no longer felt compelled to hide his alcoholism. She had been able to express her pent-up feelings for the first time the night she had addressed the *AA* in May. Those public statements brought the problem out into the open. Everybody knew about it now and she felt a great sense of relief. Before that time she had confided it to no one, not even to her closest friend, Mathilde Rochon. Grace knew that the Board of Trustees and her congregation were aware of the situation now. When questioned at church about Ray's absence, she simply replied that he was ill.

After dinner that evening, Grace had a telephone call from Mathilde Rochon.

"Grace, I'm coming over. I have to talk with you," Mathilde said urgently.

"Come on. Ray has to go out, but I'll be here all evening. What's it about, Mathilde?"

"I'll tell you when I see you. I'll be there in half-an-hour." Although Mathilde had not told her, Grace knew what her friend wanted to talk with her about. When Grace met Mathilde Rochon at the door, Mathilde was visibly distressed. She followed Grace into the living room and sat across from her. The two women looked at each other. Grace felt compassion for her friend. She knew that Mathilde loved her very much and that this was difficult for her.

"Yes, Mathilde?" Grace asked gently. "What is it?"

Mathilde began then. The Board of Trustees was up in arms. They considered it damaging to the church's image that the husband of their minister was an alcoholic. Something would have to be done, they said. They weren't going to support a drunkard.

Grace was silent. Then Mathilde said,

"Grace—I believe they'd calm down about Ray if you— would only—if you—"

"If I would *what*, Mathilde?"

"Well, if you would just go along with them a little more on—things. Addie Peoples and the Board members complain that you haven't followed through in the past on their suggestions. You know—about what sermons to give Sunday mornings, and—subject matter for classes."

"Nor do I intend to, Mathilde. Now, I've been guided by the Spirit entirely too long to allow anything like *that*. Now, if they want to do it their way, they may do it their way— and I'll just give it all to them and everything that goes with it. That's how I feel, Mathilde."

Mathilde left Grace's home that night convinced that she had accomplished nothing. Very likely she had made matters worse. Grace didn't intend to give an inch. She'd made it clear that instead she would resign!

She would have a talk with some of the board members, Mathilde decided. Several of them seemed to think that Addie Rae Peoples was the more desirable leader. As for Addie, she seemed not to want to step down from the pulpit with the close of summer. She certainly needed to be confronted concerning her part in the mounting crisis.

The next morning Mathilde thought it a better idea to see Hazel Brantner. Hazel was a strong member of the Board, and ought to be informed that the attitudes of some of the Board members could lead to serious trouble.

"In your eyes Grace Faus can do no wrong," Hazel Brantner threw back at Mathilde that day. "She's not giving us the leadership we want, Mathilde. And I have reservations about her handling of the money. What about the check for the Building Fund that she crossed over into the collection plate deposit? The church can't afford blunders like that."

"Oh, for God's sake, Hazel. It was caught and corrected. That was an honest mistake on Grace's part. Now let's be *fair*! Hazel, I'm telling you—if all this nit-picking doesn't stop soon, we're going to *lose Grace*."

Hazel gave Mathilde an even look. "No one is indispensable," she said.

When Grace returned to the pulpit the first Sunday in September, the congregation turned out en masse. Grace was deeply gratified. On her arrival at church that morning, the workers in the office and library had welcomed her graciously. All was well now. It was good to be in her place again, and among her own.

At the close of her sermon, the president of the Board of Trustees came immediately to the pulpit and asked Grace's permission to make an announcement.

"Certainly," Grace told him. Then turning to the congregation she said, "Please remain seated for a special announcement from the President of our Board of Trustees."

"On behalf of the members of the Board of Trustees," the president began, "I request all members to remain in the sanctuary for a meeting to settle some major issues that have come up in our church. To help us decide on the best course of action, the Board has invited Dr. Irwin Gregg, President of the First Divine Science Church and College of Denver, to sit in on this meeting. I understand he has just arrived. Mr. Vice-President, will you bring in our guest from Denver, please."

Dr. Gregg entered and was introduced to the Reverend Faus and the congregation. Then the Board president continued,

"Serious issues have come up in recent months concerning the leadership of our church. Certain dissatisfactions exist among the members regarding our minister, and we wish to resolve these by taking a vote here today to decide whether she should be retained or whether she should be replaced by our church's summer minister, the Reverend Addie Rae Peoples. We would like, sir," he said, turning to Dr. Gregg, "to have you consider these issues with us, and to help us arrive at the proper course of action by casting your vote along with ours this morning."

Grace comprehended the situation in its entirety now. She sat immobilized.

The minister from Denver rose. Turning to the congregation he said,

"When I was asked to come to Washington to attend a special meeting of this church body, I did not know it was for a purpose of this kind. I cannot stay to take part in anything like this. I have no vote. You will excuse me now, please." He walked down the aisle then and out of the room.

Suddenly Grace rose. In a clear voice she said to the congregation,

"I have no vote either." Picking up her pencil from the lectern, she walked quickly from the room.

Outside, Dr. Gregg extended his hand to Grace.

"My *dear*," he said. *"Believe* me, I had *no idea—"*

"You knew nothing about this before you came? You knew nothing about this before the meeting?" Grace asked.

"Nothing."

"Nor did I. I didn't know that you had been asked to come here. When you entered, I supposed that you and they knew what it was all about, and that only *I* didn't!"

"My dear," Dr. Gregg smiled ruefully. *"I* supposed that *you* and *they* knew what it was all about, and that only *I* didn't! Growing pains, my dear. Growing pains. Well—I'm starved! And I'm taking the Reverend Grace Faus to dinner—right now. Let's go."

After dinner Grace drove Dr. Gregg to the airport. With that day, there began a treasured friendship between them that would ripen steadily throughout the years.

Alone now, yet not alone, Grace turned in her thoughts to her beloved teacher and mentor, Nona L. Brooks.

"Truth isn't an ivory tower religion, children. We do not deny that a problem exists. But we do deny its right to exist. It has no legitimacy in Truth. Therefore we do not give our attention to the problem. We give our attention to Truth. Giving our attention to Truth reveals the Truth about the problem. And that is, that it has no place in Truth. It has no place in Omnipresence. Therefore, it has no place; and no place in us. Two concepts cannot occupy the same soul space, children. Choose to hold to the Truth, Omnipresence, God, All Good, in you and with you! Be steadfast in your holding. Then watch what becomes of your problem.

"Neither does being in Truth mean that we do not have feelings and emotions. It means, rather, that we know how to control our feelings, that we know how to control our emotions. 'Know ye the Truth, and the Truth shall make you free.'"

Nona Brooks had spoken these words to Grace and her classmates in the classes she taught in Denver throughout the years. Holding the words in her consciousness now, Grace reflected once more on the traumatic experience of the morning only long enough to deal with it once and for all:

"Father, I choose now to remove myself from that aura of criticism and strife. I will have none of that in my life. I could not serve in the midst of such a terrible pall. It is finished, Father. I trust You to lead me onward now, even as You have led me thus far. I follow with my head high, knowing that as an individual expression of Thy Perfect Consciousness I am in no way responsible for anyone's actions but my own. I am not reponsible for the actions of my husband, friends, or church. My actions are committed unto Thee. I look unto Thee. I look unto Thee and follow Thy guidance now with a clean heart and a right spirit renewed within me. I forgive them, Father. I am free and they are free. All is well between me and Thee, Father. Therefore all is well."

Grace awakened very early the next morning. She dressed leisurely, then took her before-breakfast walk. The morning lay fresh and serene about her. Its peace filled her as she moved along the familiar, tree-lined streets. She walked a longer time than usual, adjusting to her newly acquired freedom.

At home once more, she had breakfast and completed her morning chores.

"Go now."

Did she hear the words, or feel them, or both? Go *where*? Where was she to go? She bathed and dressed. She walked to the window and the words came to her again.

"Go now to your new church." The command, from within, was firm.

Go now to your new church.

New church! Oh, but how could that be? Father! I have just removed myself from my church for reasons that are very much with me still. A new church! Would not a new church react to my husband's drinking and to my methods of teaching and sermonizing in the same way as the former? What do You mean?

Grace went downstairs to the living room. She sat there in the stillness of the morning for a long time.

All right. Not my will, Father, but Thine be done. Where You lead, I will go.

She got up then and walked to the kitchen. She left a note on the table for Ray and went out, closing the door quietly.

Grace moved slowly along Sixteenth Street now, searching for a suitable place in which to hold Sunday morning services. Passing rows of buildings, she went into one after another. She found nothing. Shortly after noon, she crossed to the other side of the street to check the buildings there. As she walked along the 2400 block, she was urged,

"Go in here."

Looking up, Grace found herself at *2460*, formerly the French Embassy. Entering, she inquired at the desk about a suitable room for services, counseling, and classwork.

"I'm sorry," the woman behind the desk told her, "I have no vacancies."

Tell her that she will have, came the directive.

"But you *will* have," Grace said.

The woman studied Grace for a moment. Then she said,

"Yes, I *will* have. As a matter of fact, something should be available for you to see tomorrow afternoon. Come back then."

When Grace returned to *2460* the next afternoon she was

shown a room and an office on the second floor perfectly suited to her needs. Before leaving the building Grace signed a year's lease.

The next morning she placed a listing in the *The Washington Post* offering church services at her new location. Without a break in continuity the Reverend Grace L. Faus was in the pulpit at *2460* Sixteenth Street in northwest Washington the Sunday following her severance from the First Divine Science Church.

Grace arrived at her new church very early that Sunday morning. The room had been equipped by the management with a lectern and folding chairs. Grace opened the windows and straightened the chairs, then sat down to await the service hour.

Her thoughts were many. Just one week ago, she had been in the pulpit of the church she had established and led for twelve years. It seemed incredible that this could be she sitting here alone now awaiting a new congregation in a new setting. She looked about the stately, high-ceilinged room and studied the sculptured inserts that lined the pale green walls.

She had been in Truth twelve years in Denver as a student. She had been in Truth twelve years in Washington, D. C., as teacher and minister of the First Divine Science Church. Twenty-four years in Truth. *Two times twelve*. The number twelve seemed significant in her life. In metaphysics, *twelve* symbolized *completion*. And now she was beginning anew here at *2460*—2-4-6-0. Added together, they totaled *twelve*.

Noticing movement in the doorway, Grace looked up. Tears sprang to her eyes as one by one there filed into the room a group of faithful members from her former congregation. They gathered around her as she rose to greet them.

"We came early so we could help," Carol Bost said briskly. "Now, what can we do for our minister—and for our new church?"

"You can sit down and let me look at you—just sit down

and let me look at all of you," Grace said through her tears.

Grace's first church service at *2460* Sixteenth Street consisted of an opening affirmation of faith, the sermon lesson, and a closing meditation. There was no music. They were without a piano, without a vocalist. Three months earlier Kathryn Slagle had gone west to live in Denver. Since then guest soloists had been part of the program each Sunday. For those who gathered at *2460* that Sunday morning to begin afresh, the simplicity of the service underscored the unity, harmony, peace, and freedom that was theirs as they moved forward together in the light of Truth.

The name that Grace chose for her fledgling church was that which Emmet Fox and Henry Victor Morgan used for their respective churches in New York City and Tacoma, Washington: *The Church of the Healing Christ: Divine Science.*

Grace sent telegrams to both Divine Science ministers asking permission to use the title for her newly-formed church. Within hours the eminent Truth leaders wired Grace their consent, sending along their blessings and best wishes for the success of the new Divine Science organization.

Supportive, the *2460* management consented to the placement of a professionally-printed sign in the foreground of the building which read:

The Church of the Healing Christ
Divine Science
The Reverend Grace L. Faus, Minister

During the first week in her new location, Grace received calls for counseling and spiritual treatment. She set up an appointment schedule. At her third Sunday service she announced that Divine Science classwork would begin in October. Grace explained the scope and subject matter of the classes and invited all those interested to enroll in the fall course of study.

As the weeks went by so many duties claimed her attention that Grace had little time to reflect that, only a short time ago, she had fulfilled similar responsibilities elsewhere.

To keep her courage high she often thought of her first Sunday service at *2460*. That morning Carol Bost volunteered to serve as greeter to the congregation and her husband Jimmy served as usher. Grace had taken the chair near the lectern and just then Diana had come in, sat in the first row and, looking up, had smiled at her mother reassuringly.

After the service, Grace had walked down the aisle and stood by the door to meet and greet her congregation. Waiting to meet the minister that day was Mrs. John Goure of Pueblo, Colorado. With her was her serviceman son, Jim. Mrs. Goure, who attended Dr. Max Ballard's Divine Science Church in Pueblo, had come to Washington to visit Jim, a navy man attending gunnery school in the Washington area. She had seen the church ad in the paper, Mrs. Goure told Grace, and had asked Jim to drive her to *2460*. On the way, she persuaded him to join her for the hour service. Grace had introduced Mrs. Goure and the young navy man to Diana and the four Coloradoans talked together amiably.

In the weeks that followed a piano was donated, a pianist offered her services, and a soloist volunteered her talents. Grace was amazed at the way the new work was unfolding. Encouraged by the increase in attendance and the interest shown by the congregation, Grace expanded her activities to include a Thursday night healing service.

Jim Goure, the navy man from Colorado who had accompanied his mother to Grace's first Sunday morning service at *2460*, now attended Grace's services regularly. He and Grace's daughter Diana had fallen in love and within a few months the pair became engaged.

Another regular visitor was a beautiful woman always stunningly attired and always alone. She was Mrs. Helen Ganss, who had come to Grace earlier by private appointment seeking healing for her ailing young son. Helen Ganss had confided to Grace that her son, Harold, Jr., a hemophiliac, was prone to periodic internal bleeding and was not expected by doctors to live to maturity.

"I can't tell you how much your sermons mean to me," she said to Grace after the service one Sunday morning. "They are marvelous. I must go now. I don't want to keep my husband waiting too long."

Her husband, Helen Ganss explained to Grace, sat outside in the car each Sunday morning reading the newspaper while she attended church.

"Why doesn't he come in?" Grace asked.

"Frankly, he's disinclined because the congregation is made up mostly of women. Secondly, your sign reads *Church of the Healing Christ*. To Harold, that seems representative of personality. He's just not interested."

"But my dear, in Divine Science, we do not use the term *Christ* in the personality sense. The term *Christ* in Divine Science is used synonymously with Truth, Omnipresence, Principle. We use the term *Christ* to refer to the inner divinity or perfection inherent in and common to all men."

"That is very interesting. I must explain that to Harold. I would like so much to have him hear you—to have him attend one of your services."

A deep bond came to exist between Mrs. Harold Ganss, Sr., and the Reverend Grace L. Faus. They shared a close friendship.

"Grace, I believe in Divine Science healing," Helen stated early in their association. "I am optimistic about bringing Harold, Jr., to you for continuing spiritual treatment. I feel very strongly that great good will come of it."

Harold Ganss, Jr., was a tall, sturdily built boy. An amiable rapport sprang up immediately between him and Grace. As he grew older, young Ganss attended Divine Science services regularly each Sunday and Thursday. In his new understanding of Omnipresence, he was saved from the mortal threat posed by hemophilia.

Harold, Sr., no longer read the newspaper Sunday mornings while his wife and son attended church. He went with them to discover the Truth which had brought about his son's gain. Later, along with the earnest young Harold, Jr., the senior Ganss enrolled in the Divine Science classes; and through his ultimate dedication to Truth, he became a strong arm of the Washington Divine Science Church of the Healing Christ.

As the new church grew, Grace worked alone, depending only on her Inner Guidance, God, Omnipresence, Truth. She had no Board, no membership, no library, no staff. Her responsibilities were fulfilled independently and tranquilly.

Inspecting her shelf of newly-accumulated books and periodicals one day, Grace decided that these should become the nucleus of a library which she would make accessible to her people beginning the following Sunday.

The gesture was gratefully received. Enthusiasm for the availability of metaphysical literature was immediate and others began donating books and making monetary contributions to the library. In a relatively short time the Divine Science Church of the Healing Christ had a small but substantial, briskly-circulating metaphysical library.

Smooth as her path lay, Grace met her first obstacle at the beginning of her second year at *2460*. Suddenly she found herself without enough money to pay the rent. Turning immediately to Omnipresence, she held steadily to the Truth of her supply, and with unwavering faith affirmed that her needs — and the needs of her church — were abundantly met by Divine Providence.

Yet the money for the month's rent did not materialize. The due date for her rental obligation arrived. That morning Grace walked the short distance from her home to *2460* and went up to her office on the second floor. Entering, she closed the door behind her, sat down at her desk, and laid her head on her arms. It was time to come to terms with God.

"Now God, you brought me here. You brought me here very specifically," she stated firmly. "You guided me into this teaching and revealed Your Truth to me for a purpose. This is Your work. Now, if I am to continue in this, Your work, You must provide the way and supply the means. The rent is due today, this morning. Now if I am unable to pay the rent today, I will understand it as a signal that the work is to be discontinued, and that I should withdraw from this service."

Having placed the responsibility exactly where she knew it belonged, Grace experienced a sense of release, a feeling of peace as she continued to rest at her desk.

A knock at the door made her sit up with a start. She smoothed her hair into place and said,

"Come in, please."

The door opened. Mr. Oscar Mann, a member of her congregation, entered.

"Good morning, Reverend Faus," Oscar Mann said, smiling. "I got to thinkin' about this little church last night. You know, next to sittin' in my boat fishin' on the Chesapeake Bay, I like comin' to this church. I really like hearin' you give your talks. Now I thought I'd just drop by this morning and leave a little somethin' to show my appreciation. Here, Ma'am. Maybe you can use this." With that, Mr. Oscar Mann placed a check on Grace's desk in a sum well over the amount of the rent fee.

"Thank you, Mr. Mann. I am very grateful to you for your interest and your kind thoughtfulness. God bless you, Mr. Mann."

"You're indeed welcome, Reverend Faus. Well, I'll be goin' now. I'll no doubt be seein' you Sunday morning at service. Goodbye, Ma'am."

The door closed behind the Bay fisherman and again

Grace put her head down on her arms.

"*Thank You, Father. Thank You,*" she said softly. "*I understand now that I am to continue in Your work. I understand that I need never be concerned with supply again. I know that You support and maintain the work, and that You are in charge. Thank You, Father.*"

The work progressed steadily. Donations and contributions made by members and friends caused the library shelves and book sale tables to abound in choice selections. Attendance at Sunday and Thursday services increased, and spiritual guidance and counseling hours were maintained daily.

By April the pace had so accelerated that Grace was hard-pressed to meet the demands on her time.

At midnight of the last Saturday in April Grace fought a sense of panic. She had not had an opportunity that week to prepare her sermon for tomorrow morning's service.

Returning the telephone to its hook after completing the call she had received for a healing treatment, Grace sat down on her bed. She opened her books and spread them around her, reading in this one and that for inspiration. Yet inspiration did not come. She was exhausted. She lay back against the pillows and closed her eyes. If she could just go to sleep now! But what about tomorrow? She had no sermon ready— nothing prepared whatsoever. She opened her eyes and looked again at the books and materials strewn about her.

"*Father! Help me! I cannot receive Your people unprepared as I am! Morning will come soon, and I have no sermon, no message to give!*"

Suddenly the room was bathed in brilliant white light. In its midst stood the Christ, His garments radiant, His glorious presence filling her with peace. He spoke to her then:

"*Rest now, My Child. Go to bed, sleep. Have no concern for tomorrow. Tomorrow I will give you the words to speak. I will be with you tomorrow, even as I am with you now and always.*"

CHAPTER XIX

GRACE LIGHTFOOT FAUS, D.S.D.

Dr. Charles Patch returned to Washington in June 1947 to give his daughter in marriage to Navy man James Goure. Plans for the ceremony had been carefully made, but a last-minute hitch occurred when the Navy friend who was to serve as Jim's best man was sent out to sea the day before the wedding. At the eleventh hour, Jim persuaded Ray Faus to stand for him. Held in the sanctuary at *2460*, the wedding included the entire Divine Science Church congregation among its guests.

Charles Patch was deeply moved as Grace officiated while his lovely daughter exchanged marriage vows with the handsome young Goure.

"Diana Lightfoot Patch, the mountain baby born on Gore Creek in the Gore Range high in the Colorado Rockies, has grown up to marry a Coloradoan whose name is Goure," was the coincidence which entered his thoughts.

After the ceremony Charles' sense of humor came to the fore as the photographer, trying to keep the relationship of his subjects straight, finally gave up and asked the minister to identify the members of the wedding party. Grace did so, and the photographer attempted nonchalance as he observed the bride's father, the divorced husband of the minister, who was the bride's mother, talking amiably with the bride's step-father, who was the groom's best man.

172

The picture-taking continued as the newlyweds received their guests in the flower-filled room, now the setting of a beautiful reception.

His work completed, the photographer gathered his equipment, looked askance at the group once more and took his leave.

"Exit one confused photographer!" Charles laughed. "I can hear him now: 'I've done some weddings in my career, but *that one takes the cake!*'"

Happiness attended her days, her ways, and Grace acknowledged it gratefully.

When she visited the Golden Lotus Temple in Washington the week after Diana's wedding and met Swami Premananda of India, Grace was moved by the deep spirituality of the revered religious leader. Standing with Ray before the serene, luminous-eyed mystic, she responded to Swami Premananda's welcome with,

"It is a great honor to meet you. I have read and studied the philosophy of India with deep interest—its Bhagavad Gita and the sacred writings contained in the Vedas. Since then I have always dreamed of going to India."

"India comes to *you*," Swami Premananda replied, extending his hand in a gracious gesture.

The immediate rapport between Swami Premananda and Grace, born of a mutual regard for each other's spiritual convictions and leadership, became the foundation of a deep and lasting friendship. Considerably taller than the slightly-built Swami, Grace eventually came to call the beloved Indian mystic "Little Brother."

Ray, too, held Swami Premananda in high esteem. An avid reader of the great philosophies and religions of the world, Ray spent many evenings discussing these with Grace.

"Ray, you're a born metaphysician! You should re-assess your capabilities and program yourself for the ministry," Grace told him sincerely.

"I'm afraid not, Grace — all things considered! I do intend to write a *book*, though."

"You *do*? Ray, are you serious?"

"Yes! I'm going to call it *The Life of a Minister's Husband.* Do you think it'll sell?" he asked her, his eyes twinkling.

Grace gave him an appraising look. "It'll sell. *I'd* buy it," she said, and they laughed together contentedly.

Man of books that he was, Ray Faus spent many hours in the libraries of Washington. He took great satisfaction in researching subject matter that supported the themes of his wife's sermons. On Monday of the previous week he had come home in late afternoon and said,

"I stopped at the library today and picked up the material you wanted." He presented Grace with four volumes on Millikan, the cosmic ray, energy, and the solar system.

As Grace gave her sermon Sunday morning, Ray sat in the congregation listening interestedly for material from the books he had brought her and the context in which she used it. He took pride and pleasure in the topic, title, and substance of the sermon it introduced:

YOUR COSMIC ENERGY

"Your cosmic energy — what is it?

" 'Cosmic', of course, refers to the universe, to infinite time and space; it indicates order and harmony. 'Energy' has been defined as the ability to do work, produce action, the capacity for vigorous activity. Universal energy, then, is another way of stating what we are considering here this morning.

"When we speak of the universe, or the cosmos, we think of outer space and the vast expanse that lies around and beyond the earth. We sense that there is an Unlimited Power that is responsible for the order and harmony observable in outer space, and that this same Unlimited Power is also within our earth; permeating and penetrating every atom of the visible, physical world. . . .

"From where does energy come? There are various theories concerning this. One holds that all energy comes from the sun; that all life on this planet—vegetable, animal, and human—depends on the activity of the sun and its life-giving rays. . . .

"Consider now the cosmic ray which Dr. Robert Millikan sought to measure. This cosmic ray is able to move in and through matter and to become part of it. . . .

"When we ponder the immensity of the universe, or cosmos, and realize that our sun is just one of perhaps millions of suns of a similar type—we cannot but wonder at the microscopic being man is in this vast expanse of creation. In deep humility, David the Psalmist sang out:

'*When I consider the heavens, the work of thy fingers, the moon and the stars, which thou hast ordained; What is man, that thou art mindful of him? And the son of man, that thou visitest him? For thou hast made him a little lower than the angels, and . . . madest him to have dominion over the works of thy hands; thou hast put all things under his feet.*'

"Yes, as far back as the first Psalmist there was this same sense of wonder, this same contemplation of the awesome question: *What, in the infinitude of this universe in which he finds himself, is man?* What is his relationship to this universe, and to the Power that governs it? Is that Power cognizant of man? Can man obtain help from that great Power, that great cosmic force which whirls the earth in space and moves the stars in their orbits? What is behind this outer, visible universe? *What is man?* What is that Power which has made him 'a little lower than the angels,'—that has given him dominion over all creation?

"Having personally experienced this great Universal Power, inspired men of old have named it Jehovah, Allah, Brahma, God. Jesus called this Universal Power *Father*. 'I and my Father are one,' he stated. 'The Father in me, He doeth the works. Of mine own self I can do nothing.'

"Whatever it may please us to call it, it is this Supreme Power that unifies the universe and all mankind, making all one with all. In Divine Science, we call this Supreme Power Omnipresence; Truth; God; God being synonymous with *Good*.

"This Omnipresent Good we call God has given man of his spirit. Individual man has been given the inherencies, the qualities of God. Man has intelligence; man has consciousness.

" 'What man can conceive he can achieve.' We know this is true. Man moves in the direction of his thought; and man's thought, or his use of the One Universal Mind of which he is a part, is the greatest energy source in existence . . .

"The statement, 'Prayer is the greatest power man possesses', is also true. Why? Because prayer is the means by which we contact our Source of Energy; God; Universal Mind. Through the activity called prayer, energy from the Universal Mind flows through man's mind, making it possible for him to do the seemingly impossible. This cosmic flow of the One Mind which permeates the Universe is Divine Energy — your cosmic energy — God.

"This universal, cosmic Mind-energy is all about us all of the time, ever available to the individual, receptive mind of man. . . .

"Prayer involves us with Divine Mind, Divine Love, which is yet another name for God. Thus we are drawn to a higher level of consciousness; we evolve to a higher level of expression and experience, a higher level of unfoldment.

" 'With thee is the fountain of life!' exclaimed the Psalmist David as he came to comprehend the Universal Mind of God, flowing to him in meditation as energy, strength, and power. He was speaking of his cosmic energy; the great, unlimited Source of his life; of your life; of my life . . .

"Our Bible tells us that Jesus sometimes took himself away from all persons and all activity for periods of rest and renewal. He was renewed to the extent that at times he did not need food. One day, when his disciples had returned from going to find food for him, he said, 'I have meat to eat that ye know not of.' To what did Jesus refer? He referred, of course, to this Cosmic Energy we are considering here: the invisible Power in him which he had tapped; and which sustained, nourished, and energized him to a far greater extent than any food from the physical plane. We, too, may have 'meat to eat' that others may possibly know not of, coming to us from the Universal when contacted through prayer.

"To contact that Power, to know that Power, is to love and respect that Power. The more we love, the more we can do, the more energy we have. When we do what we do through the love of God and by the power of God, we have greater joy in doing what is ours to do . . .

"Let us, however, allow wisdom to guide us in all our doing, so that we perform comfortably, without straining or striving of any kind. Let us observe the rhythmic flow of activity and rest as evidenced in nature, and not push foolishly or drive ourselves beyond sensible limits.

"As we continue to grow in the awareness of the Universal Mind—our Cosmic Energy, our Christhood—life becomes much easier, more beautiful and wonderful for us, because we begin thinking and functioning in tune with the Infinite; in harmony with the cosmos. . . .

"We rejoice together therefore in the realization that our contact with God the Father within us is our greatest privilege, our greatest opportunity; and that great good is in store for us as we move into the Light of this Truth and abide in it. . . ."

Always for Ray Faus, Grace's presentations of scientific data combined with Eternal Truth was an illumining experience. It sent him on his way with renewed purpose, uplifted by her inspiring benediction:

"May we go forth now with the courage of the fearless Christ, knowing that the virtue of the healing Christ is in our hands; the wisdom of the loving Christ is in our hearts; for so it is."

He held Grace and Truth in the greatest esteem and aided his minister-wife by his understanding of her dedication to her profession. And when the mother church singled Grace out for its highest conferral later that summer, Ray was deeply moved. Only he, he felt, could know how richly it was deserved.

Established in 1898, Divine Science celebrated its fiftieth anniversary in August 1948 with a Golden Jubilee Assembly hosted by the Divine Science Church and College of Denver, Colorado. Ministers, teachers, students, and members of Divine Science churches and centers throughout the United States and abroad convened in that city to honor a half-century's worldwide dissemination of the Divine Science message: Omnipresence, Truth.

The Reverend Grace Faus and a representative group from the nation's capital attended the convention at which the history of Divine Science was presented, progress reports made and studied, long-term plans for the future introduced, addresses by attending ministers given, and special honors conferred.

On the third day of the convention the Washington, D.C. delegation was privileged to witness the bestowal of the Doctor of Divine Science degree on their minister. The Reverend Grace L. Faus, now *Dr.* Grace L. Faus, was cited by the Assembly for her work in Divine Science and its establishment in the nation's capital; and was presented her degree by her good friend, Dr. Irwin Gregg, President of the Denver Divine Science Church and College.

CHAPTER XX

GROWTH AND EXPANSION

The duties and responsibilities involved in directing and financing the activities of her church had grown too formidable for Grace to fulfill single-handedly. Reluctant as she was to concede this, she realized that if she were to continue to function effectively, something would have to be done to relieve the situation.

After much prayerful thought, Grace called upon six dedicated members of her congregation to come to her apartment so that they might discuss ways and means of meeting the needs of the church.

Although no immediate solutions presented themselves that evening, each of those present joined together in consciousness to affirm the needs of the church as perfectly met in Truth.

In less than a week, those who had attended that meeting witnessed the first step toward fulfillment.

"How long have you been going it alone here at *2460*, Grace—five, six years?" It was Harold Ganss, Sr., who posed the question the following Sunday while watching the crowd disperse after the service.

"Seven."

"It's time you were relieved of some of the responsibilities involved, Grace. This is too much for one person. Let's organize. We ought to call a general meeting—elect a Board —form a membership."

Grace was silent for a time. Then she said,

"Oh—I don't know, Harold. I—suppose you're right. It's gotten downright overwhelming in recent months."

"It's going to get more so as time goes by. I don't know how you've managed alone this long. And do you realize that soon this room will not accommodate your congregation?"

"Yes. Well, why don't you take the initiative, then? You're a lawyer. You know methods and procedures. Come up with a plan for organizing and we'll take it from there together."

Two months later on May 4, 1953, the Church of the Healing Christ, Divine Science, was incorporated in Washington, D.C., complete with a Board of Directors and membership.

The variety of professions and occupations represented in her growing congregation always fascinated Grace. Mrs. Mary Hayworth, personal advisory columnist for *The Washington Post*, enrolled in Grace's *Basic Principles of Truth* class. Mrs. Hayworth, in corresponding with those who sought her help in solving their problems, frequently referred individuals to Grace for in-depth counseling and guidance.

Then there was the handsome army colonel, LeRoy Nigra, who came to Grace's services only at Christmas and Easter. Colonel Nigra spoke several languages and was affiliated with Washington's South American delegation. One Sunday in September, Grace looked out over her congregation and was suprised to see Colonel Nigra. Greeting the twice-yearly attender after the service, Grace said,

"Good morning, Colonel Nigra! Is it *Christmas* or *Easter*?"

They shared a good laugh, and later that week Grace was a dinner guest at the home of Colonel and Mrs. Nigra. Divine Science came to hold interest for Mrs. Nigra, who enrolled in Grace's classes and studied with her until her husband's assignment to the American Embassy in Lisbon took them out of the country.

Mrs. Harriette Esch, supervising editor with the Federal Trade Commission, was a devoted student of Truth as taught by Divine Science and later became a contributing writer to internationally-circulating metaphysical periodicals. Mrs. Esch brought with her to the Divine Science classes her daughter Marion Potter, whose husband Neal was assistant to a United Nations staff member. After graduating from the School of Divine Science, Marion became secretary to the minister and edited the first of Grace's writings, *The Power of God in the Soul of Man.*

Grace felt especially blessed by the presence of the enthusiastic Ganss family, Helen, a secretary in the White House Press Office; Harold, Sr., prominent Washington attorney; and their young son, Harold, Jr.

Mrs. Norene Diamond, a government lawyer and writer with the Department of Labor, had been attending a church three blocks above *2460* for many years. One day the Divine Science sign caught Mrs. Diamond's eye as she passed by. *"Church of the Healing Christ.* Hm," she thought. "Well, I don't need *that* church! I don't need healing. I'm not sick!"

Continuing to pass *2460* each Sunday, Norene noticed one morning that the sign in front had been expanded to read: *Metaphysical Literature Available.* The words caught her interest. She was a voracious reader. "Now *that* I'm going to look into," she resolved to herself. "And I'm going to look into it *today.*"

Norene hurried out of her church following the service that morning and rushed down the street to *2460.* She looked over the bookcases of the lending library. Fascinated by the titles and subject matter, she borrowed a few books. Within a few months, Mrs. Diamond had read most of the Church of the Healing Christ's metaphysical literature.

Enthusiastic about the message of Truth, she enrolled in the Divine Science classes and later began attending church services.

As the months went by, Norene volunteered her time and assistance to the Divine Science literature loan and sales department. When appointed manager of the library and book sales tables several years later, her service in this capacity became her contribution to the dissemination of Truth, her own particular ministry. In cooperation with her minister, Norene Diamond established and staffed what ultimately came to be recognized as one of the largest, most complete metaphysical book circulation systems on the east coast.

Grace was deeply grateful for the talent resident in her congregation. When the Divine Science Church of the Healing Christ was selected as host to the Third Annual Assembly of Eastern Regional Divine Science Ministers, Board President Harold Ganss, Sr., worked closely with Grace to pilot a highly-praised program that evolved from the cooperative efforts of a committee which included Dr. Addie Rae Peoples of the First Divine Science Church and Dr. Florence Frisbie of the New Thought Center of Washington.

Nationally-known leaders of Divine Science who came at the invitation to address the Assembly were Dr. Irwin Gregg of Denver; the Reverend Carl Draeger of St. Louis; Dr. Clara Letsch of Milwaukee; Dr. Eleanor Mel of Boston; and Drs. Martha Chesterfield, Herman Wolhorn, and John Seaman Garns of New York.

During this Assembly the nucleus of The Divine Science Federation International was formed, a worldwide league of Divine Science churches and centers ultimately established in 1957 at a conference in Denver, Colorado.

A few weeks following the highly successful Assembly, Grace and the Board of Directors of her church received a letter from the president of the International New Thought

Alliance requesting that she serve as general chairman of the Forty-First International New Thought Alliance Congress to be held in Washington, D.C. in July 1956.

In February International New Thought Alliance President Dr. Robert Bitzer came to Washington from Hollywood, California, to confer with Grace on the forthcoming INTA Congress.

In the church office at *2460*, the affable Dr. Bitzer took a chair across from Grace and announced enthusiastically,

"Grace, the Congress here in Washington next July is going to be our greatest to date!"

"Dr. Bitzer—in all respect to the Alliance and to you—I don't feel that I can accept this chairmanship. I've never been involved in a project of these proportions. I can't coordinate a large-scale gathering of this kind! I wouldn't know where to *begin*! I—can't do it! I just *can't*!"

"Now let's remember our Basis, Grace—the One Mind! It is the Father that doeth the works. Of course you can. You *must*. The Alliance wishes it. Formerly, Florence Frisbie was our key representative here. Now that she's made her transition, it's up to you to assume the leadership in this city."

"But there's so little time! This is February, and—"

"You'll have all the support you could possibly need or want, Grace. All of us in the Alliance will work with you right down to the smallest detail. Grace, you're going to do a magnificent job!"

The chairmanship of the 41st International New Thought Alliance Congress proved to be an inspiring experience Grace would remember always. She met and worked closely with the leaders of other New Thought Groups in the Washington area to present a brilliant Congress attended by more than 800 delegates from all over the world.

During the opening session, Dr. Irwin Gregg, President of the Divine Science Church and College of Denver, Colorado, was presented with the key to the city, the first non-political figure in Washington, D.C. history to receive this honor.

Dr. Raymond Charles Barker of New York, whose most-recently published book, *Treat Yourself to Life*, was being acclaimed in New Thought circles, highlighted the list of speakers at the Congress.

Acknowledgment of the successful week-long convention, held at the Statler Hotel in Washington, was made through a descriptive article in July 6, 1956, issue of *The Washington Evening Star:*

". . . In other closing business this morning, the International New Thought Alliance Congress reelected both the INTA President, Dr. Robert H. Bitzer of Hollywood, California, and the Vice-President, Dr. Mabel V. Carrell of Louisville, Kentucky. Dr. Grace L. Faus of the Church of the Healing Christ here was elected regional president for Maryland, Virginia, and the District of Columbia. She succeeds the late Dr. Florence Frisbie, head of the New Thought Center here before her death in February."

CHAPTER XXI

THE GEORGETOWN CHURCH

Metaphysically symbolic of group completion, the number *twelve*, this time multiplied by two, again presented itself to Grace in 1956, her twenty-fourth year as Divine Science minister in Washington.

The year proved dynamic throughout.

From the very beginning of her ministry, it was Grace's desire never to put her people in debt through the purchase of a church site. When the Church of the Healing Christ felt the pressing need for larger quarters in 1955, Grace held to her wish for a debt-free congregation more strongly than ever.

Together, minister and Board members began investigating locations offering more space. They explored possibility after possibility. When they had exhausted their search, they found themselves back where they started. During an evaluative meeting at *2460*, Grace and the Board committee checked off one prospect after another as too costly; binding; remote; inaccessible.

At last through the inspiration and initiative of Board President Harold Ganss, Sr., Grace's wish miraculously came true in November 1956 in the Georgetown section of Washington.

It was a gem of a church, set in a triangular lot and accented by a classic spire. Styled in English architecture, it stood in simple dignity, its brown-buttressed, ivory-stuccoed walls lined with slender Gothic windows of rich stained glass and its grounds neat with well-placed shrubs and trees. Yet to Grace and her Board of Trustees, the church's most attractive feature was its space offering. Here at 2025 Thirty-fifth Street and Wisconsin Avenue in northwest Washington, the Divine Science church congregation could grow and expand comfortably.

Formerly the church had been donated to the Methodists by a prominent Georgetown family so long as that denomination continued to hold services in it. The structure had fallen into virtual disuse when the Methodists outgrew it and built a larger church a few blocks north on Calvert Street.

Returning to hold an occasional service in the Thirty-fifth Street church to prevent its reverting to the family's heirs, the Methodists were approached through the President of their Board of Directors by Harold Ganss, Sr., about the possibility of obtaining the building for Divine Science services. Harold's inquiry led to the discovery that the Federal Government had enacted a law years before to condemn the hundred-year-old church and raze it to make way for a cross-country road connecting Georgetown with uptown Washington. Further research revealed that those plans had been abandoned and that the property currently lay under the jurisdiction of the Interior Department's Park Service.

Pursuing the matter further, Harold sought out Superintendent of Parks Edward Kelly. It was during a conversation between these two practical-minded men that the plan presented itself to initiate court condemnation proceedings, enabling the Federal Government to obtain title to the property.

This accomplished, the Methodists took their leave of the building, and the Church of the Healing Christ, Divine Science, availed itself of the property for a nominal rental fee, restoration and renovation costs, and insurance coverage guaranteeing protection for the government.

News of the results of Superintendent Kelly's cooperative efforts was shared by President Ganss with the Divine Science Church of the Healing Christ's minister and Board of Trustees at their next month's meeting.

While the amazed Board members exclaimed over Harold's report, Grace acknowledged in her heart the realization of her long-held dream of a debt-free congregation.

Grace and her people commemorated the move to their new location on November 11, 1956, Armistice Day. Divine Science ministers from all over the country arrived in the nation's capital to attend the dedication service. On that day, President Eisenhower acknowledged the Divine Science Church of the Healing Christ's contribution to the spiritual and moral fiber of America with a telegram of congratulations, thrilling all in attendance.

Building modifications were financed by the membership's response to the suggested purchase of debentures, fifty to one-hundred to five-hundred dollars each at five-percent interest to be realized in five years. The support was overwhelming. The amount of money needed was raised almost over night. Renovations and installations included central lighting, new flooring, an accoustical ceiling, seating, an organ for the sanctuary, partitioned Sunday School quarters, a Board Room, rest-rooms, interior-exterior painting, and carpeting for the sanctuary and library.

Midst sawdust and strewn power tools, Don Blanding, poet laureate of the International New Thought Alliance and author of the popular book, "Joy is an Inside Job," delivered one of the first Sunday morning addresses to the newly-located congregation. In Washington for a brief stay at the time, Mr. Blanding accepted Grace's invitation to be their guest speaker, then remained to deliver two evening lectures.

Group consciousness spiraled as the weeks went by. Renovations were completed and the building stood transformed. With their fresh new look, minister, Board, and congregation found themselves attracting new responsibilities, new opportunities for service.

TIME Magazine, in its December 10, 1956, issue, featured Grace and her church in its Religion section under the heading, *Recorded Solace*:

. . . . Pastor Grace L. Faus of the Divine Science Church in Washington, D.C., . . . uses a one-minute "sermonette." *"Do we realize,"* she may ask, *"that we are an activity and creation of the mind of God? In God there cannot be boredom, fatigue, or a lack of energy . . . Let us declare that we are alive with enthusiasm and vitality for every good endeavor . . . God loves you."*

The article described Grace's Dial-A-Sermonette, introduced that year as the first dial-for-inspiration service to be offered in the Washington metropolitan area. The one-minute message, born of Grace's wish to make recorded inspiration available by telephone any hour of the day or night, was recorded on a magnetic drum and played back all day by a special machine to which a trunk line was attached. Changed several times a week, the Dial-A-Sermonette enjoyed a public response that gathered year-by-year momentum, ultimately totalling over one-hundred calls in a twenty-four hour period. Listeners of every denomination were attracted to its New Thought-engendering themes with their positive approach to life, health, prosperity, relationships, self-fulfillment, and happiness. In praise of her capsule-messages, many of them wrote to Grace, telephoned her, sought her out:

Dear Dr. Faus,

Although I am a total stranger to you, I feel that I know you.

Yesterday I stopped at your church on Wisconsin Avenue hoping to see you and to leave a token of my appreciation for your wonderful telephone service. After pausing to enjoy a few quiet moments in the sanctuary, I left my note and gift with the custodian and asked him to deliver them to you.

May God richly bless your work.

A grateful listener,

Mrs. Charles Jensen

Dear Dr. Faus,

Thank you for the Dial-A-Sermonette. I get a thrill whenever I dial and get a busy signal, for then I know that others are benefitting from your wonderful messages.

I dial as often as I can—sometimes a half-dozen times a day. One restless night I dialed at 3:45 A.M.!

Thank you for sending me the literature I requested.

Love and Gratitude,

Madeline Wengert

CHAPTER XXII

CHANGE AND ADJUSTMENT

Ray Faus was chronically ill now, requiring long periods of hospitalization. Following the move to the church's new location in Georgetown, Grace divided her time between the hospital and the church for the most part, leaving the hospital to go directly to the church in the mornings, and going from church to the hospital in the afternoons.

Then, after everything possible had been done for him, Ray was released from the hospital in late November. Taking on the responsibility of his nursing care at home, Grace carefully arranged her schedule. Each day she prepared his meals in advance and laid out his medication, then left him for a time to fulfill her duties at the church.

"Hurry home now, Grace. The hours drag by when you're gone, so hurry," he would say as she prepared to leave in the mornings.

"I will, Ray. I'll come straight home. You know I will. I always do. I'll hurry," Grace assured him.

"I'll be waiting for you," he'd add as she went out the door.

When the church closed at four o'clock Grace immediately returned to their Sixteenth Street apartment. But Ray's concept of time had blurred, and he would greet her with,

"What took you so long, Grace? How come you're so late getting home?"

She acquired a sense of urgency, a feeling of needing to hurry. Sometimes she would leave the church a few minutes early. On Sundays she would greet the last parishioner, then leave promptly, getting home to Ray as soon as possible.

The Sunday of December 9, 1956, marked Grace's first absence from the pulpit in her twenty-four years of ministry. Dick Theis, Board member and close friend of the Faus family, took her place in the pulpit. From the podium he announced to the congregation,

"It is my sad duty to tell you that Ray Faus made his transition shortly after the noon hour yesterday."

Expressions of shock filled the church. A woman who thought Mr. Theis had said *Grace Faus* cried out and was calmed by the ushers. Continuing in his task, Dick Theis followed the brief outline Grace had given him and proceeded with the service.

Swami Premananda of Washington's Golden Lotus Temple conducted Ray's funeral.

"No matter what one's religious or philosophical stand, death is a shock," Grace told her congregation when she returned to the pulpit following Ray's transition.

Without Ray, Grace's private world seemed purposeless and empty. Her ministerial duties at the new location only brought him to mind the more, serving to remind her that he had been too ill to attend any of the services there and had never been inside the Georgetown church. For nearly a year after Ray died, Grace continued to feel that she must hurry home from church. She would leave promptly at four during the week and immediately after the last parishioner had gone on Sundays, arriving home as soon as possible. Once there, she would walk through the rooms trying to grasp the fact that her husband of many years was no longer with her and that now she lived alone.

At the end of that year Grace gave up the apartment on Sixteenth Street that had been her home with Ray to take up residence in the Carillon House at 2500 Wisconsin Avenue, two blocks from the church.

From her window-fronted, seventh floor apartment in the Carillon, Grace could look southeast over Washington and enjoy a clear view of the city's historic buildings, including the Capitol and the Washington Monument. To the north stretched a wide expanse of trees, their greenery majestic against the horizon.

She was happier in her new surroundings. Her church was within walking distance. She liked Georgetown's quiet dignity and serene atmosphere; its quaint, cobblestone streets; its picturesque colonial residences backed by colorful, walled gardens; the charm and sophistication of its shops and restaurants; the beauty of Dumbarton Oaks and Georgetown University; the interesting Georgetown citizenry.

Nearby on Thirty-fourth Street lived Mrs. Jean Hill, a member of Grace's congregation and a personal friend to her and Ray. Grace had met Jean Hill at a prayer-study group in Virginia which she had attended occasionally as a guest. In the fall she invited the group to come to the church to take part in the study courses offered there if they wished. Among those who accepted her invitation was Jean Hill, who had been attending Grace's Sunday services for some time.

"I don't need to study metaphysics, Grace," Jean told her one Sunday after the service. "I've read metaphysics widely since I was a child. But I'm going to take the courses you announced today just to learn the semantics of Divine Science."

"I think that's a good idea," Grace responded.

"But I'm not going to be trapped by this, I give you fair warning!" Jean asserted seriously.

"I understand perfectly. You're interested only in the semantics," Grace stated just as seriously.

When Grace met with her new class in *Basic Principles of Divine Science* the first week in October, Jean Hill was among those enrolled in the year-long course. After completing her first year of study, Jean enrolled in the curriculum's second-year subject, then went on to the third. Midway through her fourth year, Jean Hill was, to her surprise, "trapped" by Divine Science—gratefully, happily "trapped." When she admitted this to her minister-teacher of four years, Grace laughed heartily and said,

"I knew you would be! I just knew it!"

Jean graduated from the School of Divine Science and returned as a continuing student. Several years later she enrolled in the Practitioners' Training Course and became licensed as a Divine Science practitioner. Eventually Jean was appointed to the School's faculty as teacher of *Consecration*, the fourth-year course of the curriculum which had "trapped" her.

CHAPTER XXIII

THE HOUSE OF GRACE

As the wife of naval officer Jim Goure, Grace's daughter Diana traveled with her husband from base to base, living at Navy posts across the country throughout the years. It was while the pair was stationed at Norfolk, Virginia, that Jim telephoned his mother-in-law to congratulate her on becoming a grandmother.

"If you're standing, Grace, get a chair and sit down. You're in for a surprise—a big one!" Jim greeted her exuberantly.

"All right, Jim," Grace said, reaching for a chair. "I'm sitting down now. What do you have to tell me?"

"Are you ready?"

"Yes!"

"Congratulations, Dr. Faus. You're the grandmother of *two*! Diana just gave birth to *twins*!"

"Jim—don't be kidding me at a time like this! It's too serious! Now tell me the truth!"

"That *is* the truth! I'm not kidding! *Twins!* Identical twin boys—born twenty minutes ago! James, Jr., and Jonathan. Diana and the babies are doing fine. And so's Papa Jim here!"

Several weeks later, Diana and Jim flew to Washington with their infant sons to have them christened by their maternal grandmother. Witnessed by the entire Divine Science Church congregation, the christening was a thrilling occasion, paralleled by the remembered beauty of Diana's and Jim's wedding ceremony which Grace had performed also.

Realizing that the twin babies limited her daughter and son-in-law in their ability to travel, Grace visited the young family at their assigned posts as often as she possibly could. The four brought her great joy and she loved them dearly. By the time Diana and Jim had completed their family eleven years later, they were the proud parents of eight children, four boys and four girls, all of them born in different parts of the country and all of them christened by Grace.

Grace spent her summer vacations in Denver now, teaching an occasional class in the Denver Divine Science Summer School and sometimes appearing as guest minister in the mother church. On one such occasion Dr. Irwin Gregg introduced her, saying,

"There is much talk now in state and national politics about 'Favorite Sons.' It is my pleasure to present to you at this time Denver's Favorite Daughter, Dr. Grace L. Faus."

As the house guest of Kathryn and Clarence Cobb while in Denver, Grace enjoyed a beautiful room which the Cobbs had reserved especially for her. In its privacy she relaxed with her books and her writing for two months, surrounded by the glorious Rockies she loved so dearly. Still another room was hers at *Cobb-Webb*, the Cobbs' mountain home where the three of them vacationed together for part of each summer.

Grace cherished her friendship with Kathryn and Clarence. Formerly the soloist in the Washington church, Kathryn had been one of Grace's early students and was devoted to her. Throughout the years the two women had become as close as sisters.

Grace, Kathryn, and Clarence enjoyed automobile riding frequently. Together they would drive to the higher regions of Glenwood Springs and Marble to view the spectacular scenery. One of their favorite routes was a winding highway that rose above Bailey, fifty miles southwest of Denver. Each time they neared a certain area of that mountain, Grace would say,

"I *love* this spot right here! It seems to draw me. *I love this spot!*"

They returned to it again and again. And each time they approached it Grace would exclaim, "I love this spot! It's gorgeous!"

She thought of it often, that stretch of land on the south side of the mountain, colored with columbine and dense with aspen and pine. Then one day there came the inner prompting,

"Buy it. Buy the property. Buy it and build "The House of Grace." The House of Grace!

"Kathryn, I'm going to buy that lot!" she told her friend when she saw her next. "It's where I'd like to live some day. And when I can, I'm going to build on it!"

"All right. You buy that one and I'll buy the lot beside it. We'll live next door to each other."

"I'm serious, Kathryn. I've got to have that piece of land!"

"I'm serious, too! If you buy, I will. Come on. Let's go. We know whom to see about buying those lots."

A nephew of the Cobbs owned the mountain property. He agreed to sell to his aunt and her friend the tract of land each wanted. Grace made a down payment on her property and arranged to pay the remainder on a long-term plan.

At last the day came when the land was completely hers. Together she and Kathryn Cobb owned the side of a mountain! It was a wonderful feeling, knowing that a portion of the Rocky Mountains she loved so much belonged especially to her; and in her mind's eye Grace pictured the kind of house she would build there one day.

In time she had a well dug. Then her friend Lorenzo Winslow, White House architect and student of Divine Science, offered to draw up her house plans. In less than a half-dozen years the rustic wood rambler stood complete among tall aspen and ponderosa pine, its wide windows and extending porch affording a spectacular view of the surrounding mountains. Near the walkway a pine shingle identified the dwelling as *The House of Grace*. Almost immediately, it became a summer mecca for her, her children, grandchildren, and friends.

Living close to nature on her mountain Grace spent her days hiking, gardening, sawing firewood for her fireplace, writing, reading, and gathering inspiration for the sermons she would present when she returned to the pulpit in the fall.

The wide porch beyond the glass doors of her living room had become a gathering place for mountain creatures and birds. Grace laid out food for them each morning, then watched from within as squirrels, chipmunks, rabbits, and birds of every kind and color visited throughout the day.

Waking at dawn, she would stand at the porch railing, watching as the rising sun illuminated the earth with its golden light. She stood there again at sunset, lingering to catch the first glimmer of the evening star, and often remained until the late night sky was bathed in moonlight and patterned with millions of stars.

She loved the sky, its depth, its infinite expanse of light and color; the sun and billowing clouds by day, the moon and stars by night. This she attributed in part to her father's influence. Her father's interest in astronomy had rendered him a self-styled astronomer delighting to share his observations with those around him. Grace had been especially proud of him when, at age seventy-five, he had enrolled as a student and made an intensive study of that science.

Now, for Grace, alone on her Colorado mountain, the brilliant night sky became representative of the field of her ministry throughout the years; and the stars inhabiting it, the persons who made up her congregation, individually and collectively. Like the stars, the thought of her people warmed her and filled her with happiness. She was deeply grateful for all of them and wherever she went she carried them with her in her heart. With the formidable North Star she associated Harold Ganss, Sr., whose brilliant leadership and expansive approach had helped establish the Washington, D.C. church and school as one of the strongest Divine Science centers in the world. Working closely with Harold was his beautiful wife Helen, whose warmth and light touched even the governmental realm as she went about her job in the White House Press Office. Grace remembered now attending an afternoon party at the White House with Helen during the Truman administration, walking through the exquisite rooms, sampling the chef's offerings in the kitchen, and sitting for a brief moment in President Truman's chair in the Oval Office.

Now, as always while on vacation each summer eighteen-hundred miles from her beloved Washington congregation, Grace was at peace concerning the church's summer activities under the guidance of such visiting ministers as Dr. Martha Chesterfield of New York, Dr. Lucile Frederick and Mr. Al Olinger of Denver, supported by the strong arm of Board President Harold Ganss, Sr., and his dedicated Board fellows.

The bright star of Eudora Honemond shone down on Grace with characteristic warmth and magnanimity. Eudora had first heard Grace speak during an evening lecture program at Washington's Willard Hotel. Wholly receptive to Grace's message of Truth, Eudora telephoned her the next day and asked,

"Dr. Faus, does your church accept Negroes?"

"Why certainly! *Of course!*" Grace replied. "As a matter of fact, one of our valuable Board members is a Negro woman, Mrs. Harriet Washington. And there are several others in our congregation."

Eudora began attending church regularly on Sundays, and soon enrolled in the classes. Four years later, in 1958, she graduated from the church's school, then returned for advanced study. Ultimately, Eudora's consecration and commitment to the Divine Science Principle established her as the Church of the Healing Christ's first licensed practitioner. From the beginning of her practitionership, Eudora was the channel for many remarkable healings.

A star on the horizon brought to mind the brilliant and multi-talented Mrs. Carley Dawson. Grace had first met Carley at the threshold of the church. Early one Sunday morning, finding no program of the up-coming service on her desk, Grace had walked down the sanctuary aisle to the table near the entrance and there met Mrs. Dawson. She introduced herself to the early-arriving visitor, who asked in her distinctive English accent,

"May I arrange to have a private consultation with you soon?"

The following Tuesday marked the beginning of Carley Dawson's long, intensive study of Divine Science. She had at last found the philosophy of life she had been searching for. Carley graduated from the School of Divine Science four years later and, returning for advanced study and training, eventually became a licensed practitioner. Encouraged by her minister-teacher to enter the ministry, Carley was ordained by Grace in 1967 along with Herbert H. Cole, a fellow Divine Science practitioner whom Carley called her "spiritual brother."

Winking down at Grace, a hint of humor in its shine, was the star of Herb Cole himself. The story of Herb's introduction to Divine Science always amused Grace. He and his wife, Dorothy, had attended Grace's Spring Tonic Lecture Series at the suggestion of friends. Later Dorothy urged Herb to go with her to the church services. He agreed to go with her as far as the curb, where, like Harold Ganss before him, he would wait in the car reading until the services were over. Dorothy came out of the church one Sunday morning and Herb said to her,

"Next Sunday is our wedding anniversary! What would you

like for an anniversary present?"

"I — I'd like you to go to church with me to hear Dr. Faus! Next Sunday. On our anniversary!"

"Oh. All right. That's cheap enough and easy enough!" he'd laughed.

Herb admitted later that it was neither. As he came to comprehend the Principle of Truth, he realized that it required total dedication and commitment. He enrolled in the classes.

After being healed of a long and restricting illness through spiritual treatment, study, and application, Herbert Cole consecrated his life to the Principle of Truth, becoming first a licensed practitioner, then ordained by Grace as a minister. Ultimately the Reverend Herbert Cole and the Reverend Carley Dawson were to become Divine Science teachers, and along with the young, Denver-ordained Reverend Harold Ganss, Jr., would serve in the pulpit as assistants to the minister.

Like the stars, countless men and women brought their light to bear on the work of Divine Science in Washington. The Sunday services took on added beauty and meaning through the dedicated expression of such talented Washington musicians as soloists Fleurette Joffrie, Helen Turner, Cleomine Lewis, Avon Stuart, and the church's long-time organist, Polly Zens. Always at Christmas and Easter, the special music provided by Sam Jack Kaufman, President of The District of Columbia Federation of Musicians, and the beautiful decoration of the sanctuary by Washington artist Maud Kimble and her husband Dave were a source of joy to all.

Grace rejoiced at the thought of the strength of the Divine Science Church of the Healing Christ in the nation's capital. Its establishment she was certain now had been written in the stars.

CHAPTER XXIV

FRUITION

A three-fold anniversary celebration, honoring the seventieth year of the founding of Divine Science, the thirty-sixth year of Divine Science in the nation's capital, and the twelfth year of The Divine Science Church of the Healing Christ's location in Georgetown took the form of an all-day program Sunday, November 17, 1968, and featured as guest minister Dr. Max Ballard of St. Louis, Missouri, an afternoon address by Dr. Ervin Seale of New York, a dialogue of the life of Nona L. Brooks by Drs. Lucile Frederick and Irwin Gregg of Denver, and a pictorial exhibit of the Washington, D.C. church's history.

As part of the celebration, announcement was made that an Anniversary Benefit Concert would be presented the following Sunday afternoon by Avon Stuart, noted Washington baritone who would leave the nation's capital in the spring to make his debut in New York's Carnegie Hall.

It was a great day for Grace. *"My cup runneth over! Thank You, Father!"* she inwardly rejoiced as she watched the milling crowd browse among the various exhibits.

Her cup did indeed overflow. She was blessed with a cooperative, creative, productive congregation. Through their initiative and support, Washington area citizens had been privileged to hear such distinguished speakers as Drs. H. B.

Jeffery, Maxwell Maltz, Joel Goldsmith, George Lamsa, Joseph Murphy, Frederick Bailes, Harry Gaze, Raymond Charles Barker, Tanaguchi, and Neville.

She was grateful too that for a long time now her own messages of Truth had been enjoying a wider audience through the Dial-A-Sermonette, through articles appearing in the Divine Science *Aspire to Better Living* magazine and *The International New Thought Quarterly*, and through the publication of seven pocket-size booklets based on selected sermons and meditations. Most recently, in collaboration with well-known Washington broadcaster Charles Keaton, she had prepared a long-playing record titled "Living Words and Melody." Its background music composed and played by Mr. Keaton, the recording proved to be a well-received expression.

Calling her out of her reverie as they came towards her to offer their congratulations was a trio of fellow-members of the *DAR*, which she had joined at her mother's urging. It pleased Grace to receive these friends on the occasion of her church's triple-anniverary celebration.

Then a student interested in journalism approached her with the question:

"You will write the story of your life sometime soon?"

"Oh, my no!" had been her reply.

"But your story should be written, Dr. Faus. Would you consider having someone write it?"

"Well now, I don't know! I've led a very simple life, my dear—hardly the kind people would be interested in reading about!"

Grace smiled at the tribute. She loved them all; all who had come that day, all who had come throughout the years. After the last guest had gone, she lingered alone in the quiet church, filled with gratitude for the years of dedicated service represented by those who had gathered there that day.

In the still sanctuary she sat in the end seat of the first row and recalled her good friend Max Ballard's moving sermon, "Upon This Rock I will Build My Church." Coincidentally echoing its theme, her friend and colleague Ervin Seale had spoken in the afternoon on the subject, "This Is The Church That Faith Built."

She had been deeply touched by Dr. Seale's opening remarks:

> "I suppose there are a few people in the world for whom I would give up a Sunday afternoon, a Sunday dinner, a Sunday evening at home, and Grace Faus is one of them. And that's why I'm here today with Mrs. Seale. We have loved Grace for many years, and respected her and honored her; and I do myself honor in honoring her. Besides, there are fifty in my church at the very least who are ecstatic about her. They were with Mrs. Seale and me on a cruise last May and Grace was with us. As I left my church this morning, several reached out their hands in spite of the fact that I was in a hurry to catch that shuttle, and said, 'Please give Dr. Faus my congratulations and my love.' I bring now these greetings from New York."

The day had symbolized fulfillment. Never had she experienced greater inspiration and peace than she had on that day. She had been lifted to new heights, and was prepared now to go forth with even greater zeal in service to her people.

Yet almost immediately the course of her life took on new direction.

"Set the date. Set the date for your retirement."

The command, from within, was explicit. It had come to Grace at the peak of her ministry, at a time when she experienced an influx of power and energy sufficient to keep her ministering and teaching for another twenty years. Nevertheless, Grace welcomed the command as the answer to her

204

long-held prayer that she be led to retire from the pulpit while
yet vital, capable, and strong; that she be led to step down
gracefully, confident in her choice of the person who would
follow her. She acknowledged the command gratefully:

"Thank You, Father, that You have heard me. I know You
hear me always. All right, Father. Not my will, but Thine be
done."

*"Be at peace, My Child. One will follow you in whom you
will have perfect confidence. He will carry forth your work
with power. He will be a great light. You will be led to him
and you will know him."*

In late March, Grace announced to her congregation that
she would retire from the ministry, effective September 1,
1969, and that Dr. Max H. Ballard of St. Louis, Missouri,
with whom they were acquainted, would assume the pulpit
after her.

Following the announcement of her retirement, Grace
found herself coping with repeated objections—tears, telephone calls, letters, and visits from members of her
congregation.

"You simply *can't* retire, Grace. *I forbid it!*" Eunice
Hightower, her close friend and student of many years, spoke
the words that reflected her people's reaction. Midst their
pleas that she reconsider, she held firmly to her Inner Guidance, emphasizing to them that she had been thus guided and
that she must follow the leading of the Spirit.

They rallied around her in her decision then and feted her
in May with a Testimonial Banquet. In the flower-filled
ballroom of Washington's *Hotel America*, Carley Dawson
spoke from the dais on behalf of the congregation:

"We are gathered here, one Spirit individualized, all of us
stemming from the One Mind and the One Power . . . to
honor and express our affection and gratitude to . . . Dr.

Grace L. Faus, an expression of Spirit, who . . . has to some especial degree and in some personal way, opened the door of spiritual revelation and realization for every one of us here tonight. This has been her gift to us.

"In return for what she has so generously offered to us over the years, perhaps of all the tokens of esteem extended to her this evening, there could be no more satisfying gift to her on her retirement than our joint and mutual resolution:

"That together we now prayerfully resolve, henceforward, to enlarge the radiance of Spirit which she has caused in our different lives, that we shall, by our own efforts, cause it to grow into an ever-widening Light. Not for ourselves only, but for all others who are searching, as we once searched, to help them find—as Grace Faus helped us to find.

"Our appreciation and love flow out to her now for the unique gift which has been her presence among us; her guidance, her healing, her teaching.

"We . . . give our loving and grateful thanks . . . to our Way-Shower, Grace L. Faus."

Deeply moved, Grace looked out over her people, the years she had shared with them flowing through her mind. The number twelve presented itself climactically now, this time multiplied by three. For thirty-six years she had ministered to them, taught them, and grown with them as they grew in their awareness of Truth. The guidance of the Spirit had led them to realize that the One Presence, the One Power of the universe which is God, is Infinite Good, Infinite Love; and that this One Presence, One Power, when acknowledged, accepted, and abided in, is the Jesus-proclaimed Truth that sets men free.

The End

EPILOGUE

Dr. Grace L. Faus, eighty-seven years young, lives in "The House of Grace," 70 South Circle Drive, Bailey, Colorado 80421. "The House of Grace" is also the home of *MOUNTAIN STUDIES IN METAPHYSICS*, the school Dr. Faus established in the years following her retirement from the pulpit. Here she teaches the Principle of Truth to students who come from far and near, demonstrating the power of Divine Love and inspiring all by her example.

Here, too, she writes; and has authored the booklets, *The Spirit of Joy* and *Love: The Keynote of Jesus' Teachings*. Her recently published book, *The Eternal Truth in a Changing World*, is a practical, enlightening guide to meaningful living in our rapidly changing world.

While in her mid-seventies, Dr. Faus had an organ brought to her mountaintop home and began taking lessons. Still later, she took flying lessons at an area flight school, inspired by her daughter, Diana, once a licensed pilot.

In May 1984 Dr. Faus returned to Washington, D.C., to take part in her church's Fiftieth Anniversary Commemoration of Divine Science in the nation's capital.

Affectionately referred to as "Amazing Grace" by her students, friends, and neighbors, Dr. Faus continues to illumine the hearts of all with her radiant spirit and bright smile, lighting the way to Divine Understanding for those who seek the Truth of God.

206